Writing
Short
Films

.............*Structure*
and
Content
for
Screenwriters

Writing
Short
Films

............*Structure*
and
Content
for
Screenwriters

LINDA J. COWGILL

lone eagle
PUBLISHING COMPANY
Los Angeles, California

WRITING SHORT FILMS:
Structure and Content for Screenwriters
Copyright © 1997 by Linda J. Cowgill

LONE EAGLE PUBLISHING CO.™
2337 Roscomare Road, Suite Nine
Los Angeles, CA 90077-1851
Toll Free: 800-FILMBKS • Toll Free Fax 888-FILMBKS
http://www.loneeagle.com

Printed in the United States of America

Cover design by Lindsay Albert

Library of Congress Cataloging in Publication Data
Cowgill, Linda J.
    Writing short films : structure and content
for screenwriters / by Linda J. Cowgill
       p.   cm.
    Includes index.
    ISBN 0-943728-80-0 (pbk.)
    1. Motion picture authorship. 2. Short films. I. Title.
PN1996.C815   1997
808.2'3—dc21   97-23155
                                     CIP

CONTENTS

ACKNOWLEDGMENTS

This book would not have been possible without the help of many people who, it is my pleasure, to thank here. Many thanks to:

Joan Singleton and Bethann Wetzel of Lone Eagle Publishing, for recognizing the value of this book and putting it into motion.

Ian Connor, Michael Halperin and Rhys Davies, for their insightful comments, encouragement and constructive criticism.

Diana Ritchie at Disney TeleVentures, for her fearless, last-minute help and support.

Hilary Ripps at Chanticleer Films and Bryan Gordon, for the use of the screenplay to *Ray's Male Heterosexual Dance Hall.*

Michael Kelly, at Vidiots in Santa Monica, along with the owners, Cathy Tauber and Patty Polinger, for having such a great selection of short films on video.

Ed Carter and Fritz Herzog, at the Academy of Motion Picture Arts and Sciences, for their help screening several Academy Award-winning live-action short films.

Josephine Coyle and Phil Breen, for rescuing my book from computer disk hell.

Douglas Kunin, for the use of his wonderful short *Twist Of Fate.*

Geoff Grode, for starting me on this path at AFI; Richard DeBaun, for helping me prepare; and Steve Sharon, for being there all these years.

My students at Loyola Marymount, who inspired me to take up this task.

Most of all, my husband, David DeCrane, for putting up with all of this. Without his encouragement, his perceptive comments and editorial abilities, his love and affection, none of this would have been worth doing.

INTRODUCTION

Today in Hollywood it is far easier to get an agent, producer or production executive to view a short film than it is to read a feature length screenplay. (Short form screenplays go virtually unread at studios and agencies.) The reasons are obvious. It takes less time to watch a short film than to read a script, and if it's good, it's far more enjoyable. (For our purposes, a short film generally means a running time less than 45 minutes, and usually less than thirty.)

The short film, whether made on a university campus or independently financed, continues to be a well-traveled road into the film business. Steven Spielberg, Martin Scorsese, Francis Ford Coppola, George Lucas, John Carpenter, to name a famous few, all started this way. Lucas and Carpenter expanded their student films into low-budget features; the others used short films as calling cards to production executives and producers who championed them and launched their careers. On the basis of his short film, Sidney Sheinberg recognized Steven Spielberg's talent and hired him for an episode of Rod Serling's anthology series "The Night Gallery."

The 1987 blockbuster *Fatal Attraction* began as a 40-minute short film called DIVERSION, written and directed by James Dearden. Paramount bought the film and hired Dearden to write the feature length screenplay. More recently, Elaine Holliman's short film *Chicks In White Satin* received major attention on the festival circuit. This attention led to a deal with Hollywood Pictures to write and direct a feature length version of her short.

Before these films could turn the heads of Hollywood's powers that be, they needed a strong story and good screenplay to launch the project. Without a compelling or humorous story to enhance, the visual artistry of a film becomes an end in itself.

The focus of *Writing Short Films* is on writing the screenplay for the sync sound narrative short film. This is not a manual on filmmaking, geared in any way toward production other than providing the best outline possible of principles and techniques for constructing the short screenplay. This book is designed specifically for those wanting to make a narrative-driven short film, and who recognize before production can begin a completed script must be in hand. (Experimental, nonnarrative films are not dealt with.) Though most of the examples I have selected derive from narrative sync sound shorts, these same concepts can be applied to the non-sync sound short films. Examples from Albert Lamorisse's *The Red Balloon* and Robert Enrico's *Occurrence At Owl Creek*, both essentially non-sync sound films, are used throughout this book.

Many of the concepts presented here for the short film screenplay (10 to 40 pages) are the same for writing a feature length screenplay (90 to 130 pages). But there are major differences, too. Not only do shorts differ from feature films in the size and scope of the drama, but in plot structure, too. A short film can focus on and develop the conflict in one incident to great effect where a feature film must relate a number of them and generally in less depth. For example, both Pepe Danquart's *Black Rider* and Sam Karmann's *Omnibus*, two Academy Award-winning live action short films, explore incidents on a bus in the midst of a commute. Both are less than 12 minutes long.

The principles of conflict and character do not change for a short film, but many of the rules do. For instance, a requisite for success in a feature is a sympathetic protagonist. A short film, however, may succeed primarily because it examines an unsympathetic protagonist who is fascinating. Short films often effectively deal with difficult themes longer mainstream feature films avoid.

The contemporary viewer has been conditioned for most his viewing life by Hollywood's three act structure and reality-based requirements. That makes him less familiar with the composition of a short film, visually and artistically. This allows the short-form filmmaker to take more chances. A shorter running time allows the filmmaker more freedom of expression in the sense that character can be examined with less subordination to the all-important plot of a feature. With lower budgets, filmmakers remain in firm control. Commercial restrictions that can inhibit feature filmmakers, keeping them from taking risks with their works, don't apply to the short film.

The Design of this Book

This book is laid out in four sections. Part One introduces the concepts the beginning writer must know to develop an idea, provides an overview of screenplay structure for the short film, and covers the principles of plot. Part Two considers structure in depth—the set-up, rising action and conclusion—emphasizing the tools the screenwriter uses to construct a plot. Part Three covers the writing process, with discussions on scene construction, dialogue and subtext. The final section deals with ideas for keeping a story focused. Appendices cover information on proper screenplay format, computer screenwriting programs, and more information on the referenced films.

A major shortcoming in other books on writing the screenplay for the short film is the lack of examples drawn from easily available sources. Without concrete examples to illustrate the principles of characterization, construction and theme, the discussion becomes elusive. The reader depends upon a description of events, sometimes problematic if the memory of the author fails him. Even if student screenplays are included in an appendix to the book, it is not the same as seeing a finished film. It's more important to see a film than to read one. Wherever possible, I have tried to use examples from films which are on video, several of which can be readily found in major video chains, while others can be located in more eclectic stores or libraries.

The number of domestic and international film festivals is increasing annually, and short films make up a growing portion of their programs. Each year, Hollywood pays greater attention to the festivals, both as a source of new talent, and for short form product which is in demand from major cable channels and those specializing in independent film. Many new filmmakers emerge from these forums, if not with production deals, with interested agents, producers or production executives.

Museums and university libraries and archives also acquire short films that are regularly shown as part of their monthly offerings. Major cable channels such as HBO and Showtime not only make short films as parts of anthologies, they often feature or use them as "filler" between their main presentations.

Every short film begins with a screenplay, even if it is read only by the director as he picks up his camera. Like the short story writer envying the novelist's freedom to leisurely establish mood and story, the short film writer has a difficult job in structuring his story so that the characters, theme and plot all prove satisfying in a shorter framework. This book is designed to impart a set of skills to master the craft of screenwriting for this shorter medium.

A Note on the Referenced Films

If you watch only one film while reading this book, make it "Life Lessons," written by Richard Price and directed by Martin Scorsese. It is the first segment of a trilogy of films in *New York Stories* (Touchstone, 1989). Every major video chain should have a copy of this film. Examples taken from "Life Lessons" are used throughout the book because, in addition to being readily available, it is expertly written and directed. The film is a real amalgam of Hollywood's best, working in an unusual short film format. (The other two segments of *New York Stories* are worth seeing for how Woody Allen and Francis Ford Coppola work in the short film arena, but are less successful than the other films referenced.)

Italian filmmakers didn't invent the episode film—the multi-part movie united by a single theme, writer or director—but they definitely perfected it. The Italians have lensed more short film anthologies as feature presentations than any other nation, a process they began in the 1950s. Two films I use which are readily available in most major video chains are from the motion picture *Yesterday, Today And Tomorrow*, winner of the 1964 Academy Award for Best Foreign Film. Directed by Vittorio De Sica, written by Cesare Zavattini (one film was co-written with Billa Billa), and all starring Sophia Loren and Marcello Mastrioni, these three films are wonderful examples of the shorter format. I have drawn examples only from the last two, "Anna Of Milan" and "Mara Of Rome," because they are under 45 minutes. The first film is almost an hour, and though delightful and worth a look, I consider it a little long for a short film.

Another film found in many video stores and libraries is *The Red Balloon* by Albert Lamorisse. This film won an Academy Award for Best Screenplay in 1955. The Disney Channel runs it occasionally, and one usually finds it in the children's section of major video chains. "The Dutch Master" on the video *Tales Of Erotica* is in many mainstream video stores as well.

A list of all the films discussed in this book and their video distributors is in an appendix at the end of this book. It may take a little digging to find them, but it's defintely worth it. Almost all have been commercially released, and are good examples of short films made for commercial markets, a presumed goal of all writers reading this book.

Other short films, and short film anthologies which are hard to find or have yet to be released on Video, such as *Especially On Sunday, Love Is A Dog From Hell, Boccacio '70, Love In The City, Woman Times Seven*, appear every so often on cable channels such as Bravo, Arts & Entertainment, The Independent Film Channel, as well as HBO, Showtime, The Movie Channel and the Disney Channel. Showtime, from time to time, features a trio of short films, done by major directors. The Independent Film Channel regularly shows short films during the week among their other offerings.

PART ONE

The Fundamentals

1

STARTING OUT—
WHAT'S IT ABOUT?

Storytelling is an age-old art. The first men and women to sit around the fire tried to make sense of their world by telling stories. Their myths and legends, which have been passed down and recorded, form the earliest record we have of mankind. In them we find all the elements we still use, to this day, in drama. They are:

1. A **hero** who
2. **wants** something,
3. takes **action**, but
4. meets **conflict**, which
5. leads to a **climax** and, finally,
6. a **resolution**.

From the first **creation myths** to the latest Indiana Jones movie, from "Looney Tunes" to *Lawrence Of Arabia*, these elements endure. <u>Hero</u>, <u>want</u>, <u>action</u>, <u>conflict</u>, <u>climax</u> and <u>resolution</u>. Stories are about conflict. They are told through action. Conflict results because the hero wants something he doesn't have or must solve a problem in his environment. At the most basic level, the story tells us how the hero overcomes the conflict or how the conflict overcomes him.

Getting started, even for a produced screenwriter, can sometimes be a daunting task. For a novice it can seem downright impossible. But the key to starting is simple: All it takes is a commitment to a process that follows certain steps and leads to putting words onto paper. In this chapter, we look at ways to get the process rolling by describing the characteristics of a good short film, examining its basic ingredients and defining the steps it takes to develop an idea and discover its underlying meaning.

The Characteristics of a Good Short Film

Many people come to writing the screenplay for a short film because they have an idea they want to realize. The problem lies in how to develop it for this shorter medium. A good **short film idea** is one that is focused and specific. It doesn't have time to leisurely explore more than one topic. In my experience, most story ideas for short films are too broad. They encompass much more material than can be effectively covered within this shorter framework; these would be better served being developed as feature films.

What makes a good idea for a short film, or any film for that matter? An idea should be **fresh**, something we haven't seen before. The characters should engage the audience's interest in some way, even if they don't gain our **sympathy**. It should have an affecting or **arresting backdrop** for the action to play against. The story itself should hold a few **surprises** for us as well as tell us something.

These are very general considerations, to be sure. What makes a good idea and how we come up with it is really a complex process that depends as much upon who we are as our understanding of the medium of film. But there are a few peculiar distinctions worth looking at to help evaluate and develop an idea.

Simplicity

The best story ideas for short films are relatively simple. They can be told in one sentence. They focus on one **main conflict**, sometimes only one **incident**, which is developed from inception to climax. A film may be framed by a **secondary conflict**, one of lesser importance, but the main story is most effective when it establishes its conflict early and then sticks with it. The less it veers into incidental material, the stronger the film will be. (More on this in Chapters Three and Four.)

In the Academy Award-winning live action short *The Lunch Date*, written and directed by Adam Davidson, the mere act of eating a salad becomes the central conflict on which the whole film is based. The idea is simple enough. An elderly woman believes a homeless man has appropriated her meal. The action she takes in relationship to her assumption develops the conflict and the story.

Conflict

Invariably, good story ideas for short films contain more than just the seeds of conflict: They expose a situation where conflict already exists. Conflict can be inherent in an abstract idea, a situation, an arena . . . but it must be realized in the **conflict between characters**. Characters can be animate or inanimate depending upon the story, but regardless they take on human dimensions in order for us to understand the story.

The best characters are strong personalities who oppose each other over the **story problem**. This results in unifying the opposing sides which then establishes immediate tension and creates the conflict which drives the plot. Conflict for a short film can be subtle or definite. In *The Lunch Date*, it is subtle; it already exists in the class distinction between the two characters, making them opposites. In "Life Lessons," the story of the end of a love affair between a successful artist and his assistant, the conflict between the two main characters is bluntly direct; they are opposed in every way. (More in Chapters Two and Three.)

Conflict arises when the characters are evenly matched,

or the protagonist faces a stronger antagonist and/or problem. This immediately sets up tension for the audience; they wonder how the protagonist will prevail, especially when he faces a difficult problem.

Originality

The best films (short or feature) are always **fresh** in some way. Although it seems like we've seen countless action films, fish-out-of-water comedies, and family dramas in our viewing lives, a fresh set of characters dropped into a familiar arena can give new life to an old genre. Think of Riggs, the suicidal cop (played by Mel Gibson), in the first *Lethal Weapon*.

Content based on ideas never before explored on film (or any medium) will give a decidedly original quality (*The Crying Game*). A new point of view toward an old subject may create the feeling of freshness (*Unforgiven*). A familiar plot line boasting an innovative filmic style can do the trick with a familiar plot line (*Raising Arizona*). The **combination of genres**, a comic western (*Blazing Saddles*) or a murder mystery raised to the level of tragedy (*Chinatown*) can make us see with new eyes again.

Considering the originality of an idea up front can save hours of reworking later on. The question all good filmmakers ask is, "What is new and different about my story?" Only you can discover your original vision.

Filmic Qualities

It should go without saying that all good films must be filmic. They have to be more than talking heads: They must be **visual**. This means a good narrative film must take advantage of the remarkable properties which distinguish it from other narrative media. Novels, short stories, journalism, plays, situation comedies and radio theater rely on the written or spoken word to communicate story and express meaning. The power of film lies in it using both sound and image to tell a story.

Film differs specifically from these other forms of expression in several important ways. First, we cannot stress enough the **power of images**. What we see strongly affects us all, consciously and unconsciously. The old saying, "A picture is worth a thousand words," applies because our brains are capable of processing **visual information** more quickly than **verbal information**. Film allows us to get closer to our subject than a play does. Film shows it in much greater detail, in a shorter period of time, and recreates a sense of reality on screen rather than simply suggesting it. A filmmaker can define an environment as completely as his talent allows. When his choice of images transfers a believable universe onto the screen, the audience becomes more available to him and the story he tells. If we're shown a world which mirrors our reality, or truly creates its own, we are more apt to accept the story which inhabits it. This helps us enter "**the world of the story**" because it creates a sense of a "real" backdrop for the experience.

In another Academy Award-winning live action short, *Franz Kafka's It's A Wonderful Life*, writer/director Peter Capaldi uses what is clearly a model of a towering cluster of gothic houses and apartments. As the camera ascends the model, toward a lighted window at the very top, foreboding music plays. Inside the cold, austere room, Franz Kafka (played by Richard Grant) perches at his desk, pen in hand, paper before him, struggling to compose the first line of his book. "Gregor Samsa," he says as he writes, "awoke one morning from uneasy dreams and found himself transformed into a gigantic . . . a gigantic . . . what?" he asks. Clearly upset, he casts about the room, at the furnace vent, the clock, the window. His gaze falls upon a bowl of fruit. Suddenly, his eyes light up. The film cuts to black and white, showing a man writhing beneath a blanket until uncovered. He is a gigantic banana! By the time we return to Kafka's room, he is already crumpling the paper, tossing it to the floor where it joins a host of other aborted attempts.

The world created by Capaldi is clearly at odds with our own. But through the effective use of humor and visual images, the audience accepts the "reality" of it and enjoys the story which examines and pokes fun at the creative process.

Another key factor which distinguishes film is its **fluidity** or **movement**. Movement can be understood in three ways: The **movement of character** (**action**), **movement through space**, and the **manipulation of time**.

On film we record the actions of characters. In order for characters to be interesting to an audience, they must do something, take action which has consequences the audience can understand. What action a character takes defines who he is, and this is paramount to understanding narrative-driven filmmaking. (We cover this in more depth in Chapter Two.) In a novel we can be told what happens in a story, but in film we see it happening. It becomes a **record**, a truth. The story in a narrative film unfolds through time. We <u>see</u> it, not merely <u>hear</u> it being told. Watching it unfold through the **actions** and **counter-actions** of the characters involved in a good film makes us take an active interest in the story. We wonder what will happen next. Our minds try to figure it out without our even knowing. We ponder the open-ended question until we hear a satisfying answer. Watching the characters struggle to find what they want, we become more involved with them. We root for those trying to accomplish something and are disaffected by those who don't.

Movement through space and time is also a specific property of film. Unlike narrative painting which is also organized around a dramatic idea shown in space, narrative film shows the whole story, not just one static moment of it (e.g., "The Last Supper" vs. *The Last Temptation Of Christ*). In film, the audience occupies the place of the camera and sees events as the filmmaker wants them to be seen. As the filmmaker moves his camera, we move through the story, encountering character and plot in ways that play as vividly upon our senses as engage our intellect in our search for meaning. Camera position and movement can significantly enhance our perception and experience of screen events, intensifying emotions such as alarm or elation. **Expressive motion** can draw us into a scene or pull us out of one. It can express exaltation and freedom, or indicate danger or confinement.

Take, for instance, the Academy Award-nominated live action short "The Dutch Master" from *Tales of Erotica*, written by Susan Seidelman and Jonathan Brett (and directed by Seidelman). On a chance visit to New York's Metropolitan Museum of Art, Teresa (played by Mira Sorvino)—a working-class dental assistant with repressed pre-wedding jitters—becomes fascinated with a 17th century Dutch painting. Every day, she goes to look at the painting, enraptured by the sensuality of the scene, and a young man in it. As her friends, boss, fiancé and parents all become increasingly baffled by her behavior and recount their versions of events as on-screen commentators and off-screen narrators, we witness why her fascination has taken hold: She is able to enter the painting. Through the use of expressive camera movement and exquisite lighting, and enhanced by music, we feel the wonder and the reality of Teresa's experience with her.

How the filmmaker uses his **tools—space**, **light**, **color**, **sound** and **time**—again depends upon his talent. But the original blueprint—the screenplay—must include ample opportunity for the filmmaker to capitalize on his visual expertise. The **filmmaker's tools** are similar to those of the painter. He uses space, light and color to create affective images. With the addition of time and sound, he expands the reach of those images to tell a narrative story. The ability to intercut instantly between geographical locations and time frames (past, present and future) opens up a film editorially to endless possibilities. The dynamic created by juxtaposing present and past, or jumping from city to city, can keep a film unexpected and compelling. Again, since we move through a film encountering with the characters a wide range of experiences and feelings, shifting between times or places to tell a story can produce startling results.

If, to understand the plot of our story idea, we will need a great amount of explanation in dialogue, the idea may be better suited as a play, short story or novel. Even in a short film, the **visuals** must carry the story more than the dialogue; the story must be told through action. (What are the characters doing? What actions do we see them take which further the story?) The often quoted rule is: "**Show—Don't Tell**," and the screenwriter as well as filmmaker must take this to heart.

The short film *The Red Balloon*, written and directed by Albert Lamorisse, mixes the real and fantastic with Academy Award-winning results. With little dialogue, it tells the story of a young boy who finds a red balloon on his way to school and what happens as a result. Actions and conflict carry the content and convey the magical odyssey Pascal takes because of the balloon.

The same is true of *The Lunch Date*. It has little meaningful dialogue. The story grows out of the class differences between a wealthy dowager and a homeless black man. After the woman misses her train in Grand Central Station, she kills time and buys a salad, sets it and her packages down at a table, then goes back for a fork. When she returns, a black man is sitting in her booth and eating her meal! "That's my salad!" she says indignantly. The man laughs at her, right. She sits down and tries to take it back, but he won't let her. Piqued, she attacks the salad, spearing lettuce with her fork as if skewering him. He doesn't bat an eye; he even chuckles at her. When the salad is just about gone, he gets up, returning with two cups of coffee. Surprised, she accepts the coffee and they share a friendly moment. Her train is called and she leaves suddenly. The man appears sad. Walking through the station, she remembers her packages and hurries back to the cafeteria. The table is uncleared, but the man is gone and so are the packages. Terribly upset, she paces, trying to decide what to do, and as she does, she passes by the next booth where her untouched salad and bundles still sit. When she sees them, she breaks out in laughter. She can't believe what she's done. The film ends as she makes her train, her demeanor changed by her encounter. The conflict is based on her assumptions, and her aggression is demonstrated through her actions.

Though the story essentially takes place in one location, the cafeteria in Grand Central Station, this short film does not rely on dialogue but stays on the characters' actions and reactions to drive the plot. Through editing, crucial information is withheld (the salad at the next table) until the filmmaker wants to reveal it to make his dramatic point. Told from the woman's point of view, the simple story (and short, at ten minutes) exposes our assumptions about people and how wrong they can be. The meaning is communicated visually, not through dialogue. This brings us to:

The Deeper Meaning

All great films, whether short or long, have a broader **subject matter** than just the story line the writer wants to illustrate. This is the **theme**, the underlying unifying idea. Themes are concerned with universal concepts, issues and emotions. Love, honor, identity; compromise, responsibility; ambition, greed, guilt, etc., are all experienced and shared worldwide. The universal quality of these ideas and emotions helps insure the audience will relate to the material on a level deeper than just the plot.

Without a theme, a film is an aimless story, having little significance for the audience. Without this unifying ingredient, there is no purpose, no meaning to the work. The theme is the ultimate subject of the film. Good triumphs over evil, love conquers all—though broad, these tell someone's point of view about the world.

"Life Lessons" in *New York Stories* tells the story of an extremely talented and successful New York artist at the end of a love affair with his personal assistant. The broader subject of the film concerns romantic self-indulgence and artistic self-absorption. In the Academy Award-winning collection of shorts, *Yesterday, Today And Tomorrow* directed by Vittorio De Sica, the episode entitled "Mara Of Rome" written by Cesare Zavattini, is ostensibly about a prostitute's encounter with a young seminarian. The ultimate topic, however, is the power of faith and love. Jane Campion's short film, *Peel*, is a tale about what happens to a man, his sister, and his son on their way home from viewing a property. Its real significance has to do with our inability to communicate even within our families.

It is not essential to have the **theme** completely worked out when you begin, but it must be by the final draft. Themes may emerge or change in the process of writing. It may take several drafts before you discover your theme, but whenever your theme emerges, it is best to let it help unify the story. The closer your story stays to its theme, the easier other choices related to it will be.

Themes grow out of who you are and what you believe. The best come from your emotions, experiences and insights about people and the world. For a theme to be compelling to an audience, it must first have compelled you in some way: To understand, to believe, to share, to tie your individual beliefs to a collective ethic. It must be important to you. You must believe in it; if you do not, no one else will.

A few questions can help define and clarify a **theme**. Ask yourself:

1. How does the story speak to me?
2. Does it represent my best dreams or worst fears?
3. Is there something innately **universal** suggested in the material?
4. Are there **archetypal relationships** in the material, i.e., mother/daughter, father/son, mentor/student, whether the characters are related or not?

If you know the story's ending, even only conceptually, then put it together and see what it says to you. Ask:

5. Who is destroyed?
6. Who grows?
7. What causes the destruction or growth?

8. If the hero wins, what special quality enables him to overcome the opposition?
9. Did he have it at the beginning?
10. If not, then how does he get it?

If the protagonist falls in love and spends the rest of the screenplay trying to capture the object of her affections, then your story is about love. But what kind of love? Is it a romantic infatuation which may deepen over time? Is it an obsession which will lead to disaster? Be as specific with your theme as you will be with individual plot considerations.

The topic of theme is always controversial. How it comes into being, when and who defines it, whether it is important at all, have all been debated. Films are first and foremost entertainment. But even in comedies, whose purpose is to make us laugh, the best ones always comment on our condition. Stories are always about something and the more conscious the writer is about what he is saying the more powerful the pull of the message and the more effective the film. But don't beat anyone over the head. A good rule is to think of your **theme** as another writer's tool, not a message to be conveyed by your work, even though that is the ultimate goal.

Where To Begin?

Depending upon the creator, ideas which serve as the basis for short films evolve in different manners. Actual events seen on the evening news or read about in the morning paper might provide the inspiration. A person one has met or a situation one has encountered can spark an idea. Dreams can provide an original source from which to draw.

Originating Ideas

Although basic, it is worth examining the six areas from which most originating ideas arise.

1. **Character**. We've all met people who are fascinating to us in one way or another. Perhaps it is what they do or how they do it that interests us. Perhaps it's what they

13

know. Something in their personalities draws us to want to understand them. Human action forms the core of drama. Because human behavior fascinates, people are the most obvious starting point for a writer.

Most short films are, in fact, **character pieces**. They focus on a character by allowing his behavior to show who he really is ("Life Lessons," "Mara Of Rome"). "Character piece" is a term used to describe a story that is thought to have little plot, but all the best stories in every genre are **character-driven**, and not plot-driven. Your idea for a short film may not be originally propelled by the need or desire to study one or more characters, but no one element of your screenplay's success is ultimately more important. Think about your characters as soon as you start your idea. They will help you as much in developing your idea as in telling your story.

2. **Environment**. Certain human behavior tends to occur in specific places. Different places attract different people. Stock car races take place in one environment; a game of croquet occurs in another. Place also relates to mood. Because environment contains specific activities, writers can use place to generate germinal ideas.

3. **Incident**. An incident is a rapid change in circumstances for one or more people. It usually has to do with events and deeds, either active or passive; someone does something to others, or something happens to him. Although incidents can be gentle or violent, for a writer the most productive are life changing. The change in circumstance should involve highly contrasting conditions. The film *Trading Places* is a perfect example of this in the extreme. But many short films explore a strong incident, as in *The Lunch Date*, *Black Rider* and *Omnibus*. Incidents always contribute to story in a drama. Simply defined, story is a sequence of incidents.

4. **Abstract ideas**. Using philosophical or thematic ideas as the starting point for a screenplay does not necessarily mean the film must be didactic, although this is always a danger. The beginning thesis can be suggestive

of the other elements, such as plot and character, and does not have to control the whole structure. The writer, though, needs to avoid themes which have been overused and overworked or ones that he does not fully understand. He would need to proceed cautiously if his theme were, for example, how greed leads to disaster, and he had not yet imagined unique characters or a novel way to illustrate his idea.

5. **Situations**. This can be defined as a relationship within a certain set of circumstances. One example might be the prostitute and her pimp. Relationships that are locked together on an emotional level deliver the best potential material to writers. Thus, a prostitute and pimp who need each other emotionally and form a kind of family could make a stronger story than two characters who aren't emotionally involved. Contrasting individuals within these circumstances makes possible colorful situations.

6. **Informational Area**. This consists of areas about which the writer wishes to communicate information, i.e., homelessness, terrorism, the holocaust. **Research** follows in painstaking detail. Historical material can be a great source of ideas for writers.

Once the idea emerges, the writer must shape and expand it with elements which will contribute to the story and screenplay. Asking these questions will help you begin:

1. Who will the main characters be?
2. What are their relationships?
3. Where is the conflict?
4. How does the conflict erupt?
5. What drives the action of the story forward?

Sketching out the **motivation**s and **backstories** of the main characters helps make the idea concrete. Describing time and place lends specificity to the world of the story. Writing down your initial thoughts on the arrangement of the material will aid the process of organizing scenes later. Compiling a mass of miscellaneous notes will support the whole endeavor. Remember, for the writer, ideas remain abstract until written. Just writing down incidental notes to yourself will start the process of putting ideas to paper. You already will have begun your script.

Research, Belief & the World of the Story

The **world of the story** is not just the setting or the back-drop against which the characters act and the film takes place. It is the feeling that the space delimited on the screen extends beyond what we actually see; that the lives of the characters inhabiting this world continue when they are out of view, that the world created and shown is part of a larger world. This world outside the camera lends the work a feeling of authenticity.

At the same time, it is important to understand that the world in the screenplay or film is not a real world but a representation of one. Though this distinction is obvious, it needs to be pointed out time and again. What happens on the screen is a portrayal of characters and events, not real life. The audience knows this, but desires nothing less than to lose itself in the events happening on the screen. To achieve this, the audience must **willingly suspend disbelief**. This willingness of viewers to suspend doubt about the "real truth" (that what they are watching is fiction) makes it possible for them to fully accept imaginary creations during the time span of the film. But it is only possible if what they see happening on the screen feels true and credible.

Achieving truth and **credibility** in drama is a multidimensional task. It starts by making sure you understand the arena you are writing about. If one of your characters is a gourmet and your idea of cooking is opening a jar of ready-made pasta sauce, it is obvious you need to do a bit of research in order to bring this character and her world intelligently to life. If you are writing about an abusive relationship, interview therapists, victims, perpetrators. Delve particularly deep into case studies, which offer a key to how characters create a situation, conflict and push a story.

If your story is set in Africa and you have never been there, research it. Read books, rent documentaries, try to find people who have been there and can tell you about it. Go, if you can (or maybe find a place a little closer to home).

Research is a writer's best friend. Out of it come twists and turns, obstacles and complications impossible to imagine, little details that give the screenplay authority and this feeling of authenticity. It only comes from knowing the material. If research is skipped over, the work often seems superficial, familiar or, worse, phony. The screenplay and film must feel real or it won't succeed. Researching it well is the first step toward making it happen.

From Idea to Story

The evolution of ideas into screenplays has as many routes as there are screenwriters, and every writer must find his own best approach. But no matter how different, ideas generally develop through these stages: concept, character and conflict.

Concept, Character & Conflict

The initial concept or idea for a film usually yields either a character or a conflict. Whichever it is, the other must be supplied before any real development can take place. If the idea revolves around an interesting character, the writer must invent a problem or conflict in order to reveal what makes this character interesting. The same is true if the starting point is a conflict. The writer needs to create a character who will take action and best exploit the conflict of the story.

Sometimes the beginning concept is not developed enough to produce either character or conflict. In this case, the writer may do a couple of things to get moving. She may research the backdrop of the concept, hoping to discover in the process a springboard to either a character or a conflict. Or, after researching the area, she may ask questions about what interested her in the first place about the idea, hoping to find any tension around the concept to expand into a conflict. If nothing occurs to the writer, it may be best to look for a new idea.

Short films and features depend upon conflict to work. It is primarily the struggle between opposing forces which holds the audience's attention. We will discuss the other factors that contribute to drawing us into successful films later, but conflict is the starting point. Without tension, audiences lose interest. Conflict equals drama.

Five Questions That Won't Go Away

To develop the story, key elements need to be defined. The following five questions will help you monitor your story and keep it focused. Think about the answers to these questions as steady feedback—information you need in order to know how you are performing as a writer. As the story evolves, don't be afraid if the answers change. These mutations usually signify greater development and deeper meaning.

1. *What is it about?* Initially, the answer may involve only the **subject matter** of the story. But as the writer works with the material, a broader subject should emerge. This is the **theme**, the underlying meaning of the screenplay, what you are saying about life.

2. *What is the* **genre**? There are basically five types:
   a. **Comedy**
   b. **Farce**
   c. **Drama**
   d. **Tragedy**
   e. **Melodrama**

In **comedy** (*Mrs. Doubtfire, Tootsie*) and **drama** (*Shine, Jerry Maguire*), the central motif is the triumph of the hero over adverse circumstances resulting in a happy ending. In comedy the story is humorously told. **Farce** is ridiculous, exaggerated comedy based on broadly humorous situations (*Ace Ventura: Pet Detective, The Nutty Professor*). Its only intent is to be funny. **Tragedy** refers to any work dealing with somber themes, leading to a disastrous, catastrophic conclusion (*Chinatown, Glory*). **Melodrama** intensifies sentiment and exaggerates emotion, action and plot over characterization (*Twister*, *Cliffhanger*).

There are numerous **sub-genres**: **western**, **thriller**, **action**, **murder mystery**, **science fiction**, **fantasy**. Most fall under the heading of **melodrama**, though a few may be considered drama or comedy in their own right. Most short films fall into the first four categories. Time considerations do not usually permit the development of a complex plot like that found in melodrama. Also, as we'll see in Chapter Two, the best short films rely on effective characterizations.

Defining the genre usually implies finding the right tone of your film. If it's a comedy, is it dark and satiric like *The War Of The Roses* or more rooted in reality like *Tootsie*? Is it a romantic fantasy like *Pretty Woman*? **Satire** creates a distance between the viewer and subject. **Realism** tends to bring us closer to the characters.

3. *Who is the protagonist?* This is the main character. The next chapter will discuss this character in greater depth, but for now think about the protagonist in these ways: Who is the character fundamentally, and why is he involved in this story now? What does he want and why? What the protagonist wants relates to the plot of the screenplay; to plot an involving story, we must know what the main character wants. "Why" the character is involved in the story relates to his motivation.

4. *What is the driving action of your story?* The **driving action** originates in an **event** or **incident** that serves as a **catalyst** for the story. The catalyst focuses the protagonist on his goal. It causes the protagonist to act. The protagonist's action should always drive the story forward. What the protagonist wants to accomplish draws or pulls the character forward, why he wants it (motivation) pushes him. The structure for the story comes from its driving action.

5. *Who or what opposes the protagonist?* This opposition provides the **main conflict** of the story. The main conflict is the **primary obstacles** which stand in the protagonist's way. If the conflict is represented by a person, referred to as the **antagonist**, the same questions apply to her as to

the protagonist. What does she want and why? If the antagonist is as committed to her goal as the protagonist, the conflict will be stronger and the audience will be more interested in sitting through your film until the last frame.

Many beginning writers resist personifying the antagonist. Either they don't want to commit to one specific antagonist or they don't see a person in that role. In a short film, the antagonist doesn't have to be "evil" or "mad;" the antagonist in a short film is generally the character opposing the protagonist in the pursuit of his want.

You cannot have a story without conflict. Action and conflict are the starting points of construction.

Development

As previously stated, the basic formula for a short or long film is:

1. A **hero** who
2. **wants** something,
3. takes **action**, but
4. meets **conflict** which
5. leads to a **climax** and, finally,
6. a **resolution**.

This incredibly broad plan for construction can be amplified or modified in many ways. But because it is so broad it becomes a generous starting point.

Once the key elements have been defined, the writer may start developing a rough, overall story plan. Using the formula above for reference, the plan should break into three simple, almost rudimentary parts: beginning, middle and end. The beginning sets up the story by introducing the protagonist and establishing the dramatic problem or conflict. In the middle, the protagonist faces progressive complications as he attempts to reach the goal. The end focuses on how the conflict is resolved.

Again, all else flows from the clear goal of the protagonist. The tougher the obstacles he encounters in the quest for his goal, the harder the protagonist must work, and the more interesting the story will be.

Entertainment & Inspiration

Any story, whether written or filmed, long or short, must succeed first and foremost in garnering and holding the audience's interest. To be successful, it must entertain on some level. To entertain means to hold one's attention; to divert; to amuse. Entertainment does not always have to be happy or amusing; but it must be potent. Entertainment succeeds when it removes the viewer from his own life and involves him in the story he is watching.

All writers must determine what is interesting about the stories they want to tell, and what has the potential to grab viewers. A strong film needs to be fresh, unique and different so audiences won't feel they have seen it before, even if the basic tale has been told a hundred times. How many different ways are there to create a romantic comedy? The basic ingredients are almost invariably the same (boy meets girl), but original-thinking writers are able to continue concocting stories that keep the genre alive and audiences entertained.

Guy de Maupassant put it this way when discussing the purpose and effect of a story:

> "The public is composed of numerous groups who cry to us [writers]: 'Console me, amuse me, make me sad, make me sympathetic, make me dream, make me laugh, make me shudder, make me weep, make me think.' "

This is our job: To entertain, inform, move and inspire. We entertain by creating amusement and surprise; we inform by having something new, relevant and/or important to say; we move by arousing the emotions; and we inspire by showing ennobling action. Remembering these story goals helps when we begin to create and develop the plot. Just as the protagonist has goals, the storyteller has them, too: To stimulate the audience's curiosity about the character or situation, and then engage its emotions.

Exercises

Screen "Life Lessons" from *New York Stories, Occurrence At Owl Creek*, or *Peel*.

1. Identify the underlying concept of the film.
2. Identify the main conflict for the protagonist.
    a. What does the protagonist want?
    b. What stands in his way?
3. Jot down a few sentences describing the basic story conflict as that conflict progresses from its inception to its climax and resolution. Make it a very general description of the basic story idea, not a detailed account.

Now, take your idea and jot it down in a few lines or a few paragraphs. You might start by defining a backdrop or situation or character. Examine your idea with an eye to turning it into a workable concept. Focus on the main character and the central conflict (problem) this character faces.

For example: You're interested in dance and you want to use this backdrop in a short film. You have an idea about a young tap dancer who admires a beautiful ballerina at his dance school. Here you have the germ of an idea. The tap dancer admires the ballerina, but how does she feel about him? Does she know of his feelings? Does she even know he exists? If the tap dancer secretly admires her or is too shy to declare his feelings, and the ballerina is so beautiful as to seem unapproachable, we now have described a problem for the protagonist. Implicit in this is the action the protagonist must take: he somehow must connect with her. How and what happens becomes the plot, dictated by what you are trying to say.

Now, remember that formula? **Hero**, **want**, **action**, **conflict**, **climax** and **resolution**. Using this, determine what action the hero takes, what resistance (conflict) he or she meets, and how the action builds to an unexpected climax. You don't have to have all the specifics yet; think in broad terms.

2

CHARACTER & EMOTION— WHO DOES WHAT AND WHY?

Characterization in film differs greatly from that of prose fiction. In novels and short stories, the author can describe the protagonist and other characters in minute detail, telling the reader everything important to know about them. The **omniscient voice** most novels employ also helps to establish exactly who the characters are in the reader's mind.

In film, the screenwriter doesn't have the luxury of time to tell the audience about the character. The emphasis in film is on **showing**. The screenwriter must rely on **action** and **behavior** to show the audience who the character really is. This is as true for a feature film as it is for a short film.

Film differs greatly too from theatrical plays. While playwrights follow a structure somewhat analogous to the screenwriter, dialogue plays a proportionately greater role on the stage because action is limited by the proscenium arch. The world on the stage also tends to be more symbolic and artifical than in film.

Creating multidimensional characters probably can be described as one of the more (if not the most) difficult tasks a screenwriter faces. Often, the idea for a screenplay begins with an arena or backdrop, a situation or event. Rarely does it originate with an emotionally riveting character. Characters are usually created to fit the story, not the other way around. Yet if the characters don't ring true, the audience is less likely to accept a film on the basis of its story alone. As we discussed in the last chapter, the audience must willingly suspend disbelief and enter the **world of the film** in order for that film to fully succeed. The strongest, fastest way into this fictional world is through the main characters. In order to bring the audience along in the story, writers must create characters the audience can relate to and identify with, or at the very minimum, characters we are immediately intrigued with and want to know more about.

In this chapter, we look at what makes a strong film protagonist, methods to build characters, how to develop and reveal them in relationship to the plot, and, most importantly, ways to breathe life into them. The goal is to create characters who become so credible they exist for the reader, and then viewer, as real people.

The Relationship Between Character and Plot

In Aristotle's philosophical essay, "The Poetics," Aristotle said that men are whom they are as a result of their characters (meant here as the aggregate of a person's traits and features), but it is through their actions that they become happy or miserable. Therefore, he states, drama is not the depiction "of men (character), but of doings (action)." Because action makes up the plot, Aristotle is generally interpreted as placing the emphasis on plot instead of character. This has generated colossal debate throughout literature. It can be more helpful, however, if we understand Aristotle to mean that people are what they do (their actions), and this is the best representation of who they are. The screenwriter must always keep this relationship in mind as she constructs the plot. If every action that advances the plot is seen as an opportunity to reveal character, then the motivations, choices, actions and reactions of the characters will become clearer both to writer and viewer, and they have more impact.

In the best films, plot is character. What happens only happens as a result of who the characters are. Short films, with no time to waste, depend even more upon this understanding of character to succeed. If you recognize that your character has played a part, however small, in creating the situation he is in at the start of the screenplay, then all the resultant actions and events can be seen as externalizations of his inner world, and the whole story gains deeper significance.

Remember: Character generates and causes plot, and plot results from and is dependent upon character. Do not think of them as separate, but locked together in a cause-and-effect symbiosis, and your stories will be stronger.

The Short Film vs. The Feature

The dictionary gives a plethora of definitions for "character." In drama and film, the term refers to the figures represented in the work. **Characterization** refers to the method the writer uses to fashion these fictional creations.

Characterization in the short screenplay needs as much attention as it does in a feature-length script, if not more. Short films do not have time to develop complex plots. They seldom have budgets for special effects, exotic locales or large armies of extras. A clever gimmick at the end can take a short film a long way if it surprises the audience effectively, but these are hard to invent. Therefore, most often, short films depend on character. At their best, short films explore the principal character in relationship to another character (usually the antagonist) or the problem in the plot, and reveal to the audience something interesting and unknown about him. Sometimes the revelation surprises even the character himself. Whatever the emphasis of the story, the audience needs to feel that the main characters are real, complex people, even though we only see a small part of their lives.

Want & Need

In the book *Theory and Technique of Playwriting*, John Howard Lawson says that drama cannot deal with people who are weak-willed; who cannot make decisions of even temporary meaning; who adopt no conscious attitude toward events; or who make no effort to control their environment. In drama, characters, specifically the main characters, must be active. If they are not, the drama (film or play) will fail. The protagonist must be committed to something and forced to take action because of that commitment.

The most important things a screenwriter must know about the protagonist are:

1. What does the character **want** and **why** does he want it?
2. What does he **need** emotionally?

The **want** refers to the story goal; this creates the action of the story and gives the plot direction. The **why** relates to the protagonist's conscious **motivation**. These are the reasons he understands and gives for the pursuit of his goal. The protagonist's **need** differs from what he wants. His need refers to his unconscious **motivation**; it comes from a depth of his psyche of which he is ignorant. In a sense, it can be considered what he unconsciously needs to become whole. This is what compels the hero to act in often irrational ways.

The protagonist's conscious and unconscious motivations push him through the story, the goal pulls him.

Want Vs. Need

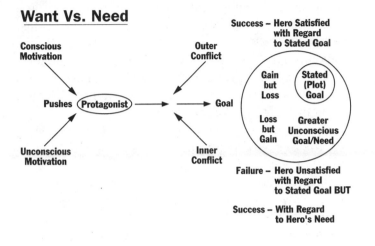

A knowledge of basic psychological principles can help the writer here. In short films and features, too, the protagonist's need often opposes his stated goal. Part of the conflict results from the disparity between stated aim and the subliminal need.

"Life Lessons," from *New York Stories*, is a good example of need vs. want. The main character, Lionel Dobie (played by Nick Nolte), is a successful artist living and working in Manhattan. At the beginning of the film we learn two things: he has no new paintings for a big exhibition of his in three weeks, and his assistant Paulette (played by Rosanna Arquette), with whom he is in love, is leaving him. What does he want, why does he want it, and what does he need?

    Want: To keep Paulette in New York

    Why: He says he loves her

    Need: Emotional turmoil in order to paint

Let's look closer. Lionel states his goal at the beginning of the movie. He doesn't want Paulette to leave New York and he tells her this. He spends the entire movie trying to convince her to stay. His conscious reason is because he loves her, and he tells her (and the audience) this time and time again. But what he really needs is turmoil in his life. He uses this turmoil to fuel his art. Is he conscious of his need? Not in the least. How do we know Lionel needs this conflict to paint? The screenwriter shows us in Lionel's response to every disagreement, dispute, and battle with Paulette. After each altercation, Lionel throws himself into his painting, with wondrous results.

In Jane Campion's *Peel*, a father (Tim) wants to prove a point to his son (Ben). Because Tim is already upset with his sister Katie at the beginning of the film, he overreacts to his son's behavior. His regressive action causes Ben to run off. Now Tim's conflict with his sister really heats up because they're stuck in the boondocks and Katie needs to be home by a specific time. What are Tim's wants and needs?

Want: To prove a point

Why: Ben is acting up (Tim actually is mad at his sister)

Need: To free himself from his rivalry with his sister

The rest of the film tells us whether or not it is possible for Tim to achieve his need.

In *Ray's Male Heterosexual Dance Hall*, an Academy Award-winning short film written and directed by Bryan Gordon, the protagonist, Sam, desperately wants a job. In order to find one, he must disregard his ideals and kiss up to self-appointed big shots and stuffed shirts. But he needs his self-respect, which is constantly assaulted as he hunts for a job lead at Ray's. Given his situation, his want and need are at odds. Finally, the brownnosing becomes too much for him and after a snub from a past coworker, Sam's self-respect wins out, and in the process, wins him a job. What does Sam want, why does he want it, and what does he need?

Want: A job

Why: Because he needs one

Need: To maintain his self-respect

Features, plays and most short films use the answers to the questions of "want," "why" and "need" to define a protagonist and to build a plot. On film or stage, characters who want something definite are more active, and therefore, more interesting than passive characters. A successful feature film must be driven by an active protagonist, one committed to achieving his goal in order for him to last through a feature's two hour length. If he is not active, the film will flounder and the audience will become disinterested.

A short film, however, can bend these rules to some degree and still succeed.

Character Need Driving the Story

If the character's want doesn't drive the story, his need must. An example of bending the rules and succeeding is Frederic Raphael's "The Man In The Brooks Brothers Shirt," an adaptation of a Mary McCarthy short story. Set in the mid-1930s, the story begins on a train bound for California. The protagonist, a cynical young New York journalist with leftist sympathies (played by Elizabeth McGovern), is on her way to tell her father she is getting married—for the second time. An encounter with a traveling salesman (played by Beau Bridges), though, forces her to face the fact that she does not know what she believes in or wants anymore. "What do I want?" she asks herself, "Mr. Right—or Mr. Left?" When the film starts, the cynical heroine thinks she has all the answers, which is what leads her astray. However, through her sexual encounter with the older man, she in fact discovers she has no answers. The film dramatizes her conflict: bourgeois security or the bohemian excitement of the good fight. Her uncertainty about her upcoming marriage, her goals, her future in general, is what she needs to face.

"The Man In The Brooks Brothers Shirt" never feels tiresome or unfocused. The main reason lies in the very goal-driven antagonist Jerry Breen. He raises the question: Can the heroine resist him, and what will happen if she can't? He makes the protagonist <u>reactive</u>, not passive. Her reason for accompanying him to his cabin—there might be a "story in it: 'Sex and the Modern Working Girl'"—gives the illusion that she knows what she's doing. Her heavy drinking, however, unmasks her unconscious motives: the alcohol enables her to check her good intentions at the door and allows her unconscious mind to take charge. It is only at the end, after her confusion has surfaced, that we understand why she put herself in such a psychically dangerous situation in the first place: Because she is unsure about her marriage and life. What does she want, why does she want it, and what does she need?

> Want: Initially, to exploit the antagonist and get a story
>
> Why: She's bored and it's hot
>
> Need: To face her confusion over her conflicting desires

The heroine's need drives her to compromise herself so that she might wake up and look at what she's doing with her life.

Finding the answers to these three questions is not as simple as one may think. Often a character's real need (the unconscious **motivation**) is as elusive and impenetrable to the writer as those of actual people. Yet if the writer keeps digging and thinking about the character, trying to discover this psychological key, he will be rewarded. A clear understanding of the character's need will usually increase the story's intensity and deepen the meaning of the conflict. It may take several drafts before the need of the protagonist begins to emerge truthfully, but it is worth the time and effort.

Defining the Character

Once you have a basic understanding of these questions you have the structural key to what drives the story. Unless the characters are conceived in three dimensions, the audience won't fully relate to them or to the story. Your characters must have emotions, attitudes, beliefs, and actions that represent them. They need history, personal traits, and quirks in order to come alive. How do we create these? Where do we start?

Personal Experience

Writers of fiction, whether prose or drama, draw from their whole background of experience to create the people who live in their stories. Good characters often come from actual models. But, as Somerset Maugham said in his autobiography, *The Summing Up*, since we know very little even of the people we think we know the best, we can't just transfer them whole-body to our work "and make human beings of them. People are too elusive, too shadowy to be copied; and they are too incoherent and contradictory. The writer does not copy his originals; he takes what he wants from them, a few traits that have caught his attention, a turn of mind that has fired his imagination."

A perceptive writer is an observant one, watching people for interesting and entertaining features, mannerisms and reactions, and then trying to figure out why they are that way. These can be conceived as clues the writer uses to reveal, on the page, who the character is. A character's idiosyncrasies and unusual behavior encourage the audience's interest. We wonder, "Why did she (or he) do that?" and we follow along, hoping to get the answer.

Basing characters on people we know well serves another purpose. It gives us an indication what a character's response might be in a particular situation. A character's response to a conflict or an accord is very telling and helps shape the audience's opinion of him one way or another.

Character Biography

Whether your protagonist looks like Quasimodo or Prince Charming, Esmeralda or Jane Eyre, appearance plays a part in defining who the character is. What part of the world he comes from and which social class he is born into also contribute to a character's composition. Psychological makeup, too, will affect how he acts. It is important to know as much as possible about all aspects of your main characters to make them come alive. Many writers advocate the use of character biographies to define the characters and help keep actions consistent with who they are. But whether or not you write down these biographies, the important information must be known to you.

A **character biography** is a description of the salient information of the character and covers both sociological and psychological background. Below is an outline of what you might want to cover in your biography. Below is an outline suggested by Lajos Egri in *The Art of Dramatic Writing*.

Physical Appearance

1. Sex
2. Age
3. Race
4. Physical Attributes
5. Physical Defects
6. Heredity
7. Bodily Care

Sociology

1. Class
2. Education
3. Occupation
4. Home Life
5. Religion
6. Nationality
7. Political Affiliations

Psychology

1. Sex Life
2. Morality
3. Personal Ambitions/frustrations
4. Temperament

5. Complexes
6. Extrovert/introvert
7. Talents
8. Qualities
9. Unique traits

This brief outline of topics, qualities, attributes and peculiarities, etc., is not meant to be solely a fill-in-the-blanks questionnaire. These headings should be developed with the idea of understanding your story better through understanding your character and her motivation**s**. How? Let's continue.

It is through our **physical appearance** that we first meet the world—or how the world first meets us. People are judged by the clothes they wear, the cut of their hair, whether they are clean or dirty, if they are healthy, athletic or deformed. How someone looks has a definite effect on how he acts, as well as on the way other people react to him. Think about the Hunchback of Notre Dame and how his appearance influenced his behavior and others' toward him. The same process works in the audience, too, as they meet your characters. Physical characteristics <u>can</u> be very important.

The **sociology** of your character is a study of his or her environment. Where a woman is born affects who she will become and how she will behave. If she's born in East LA or Eastside Manhattan, her behavior will vary. Whether her parents were nurturing or oppressive will cause her growth to be healthy or scarred. Knowing her education, social status, ethnic background, religious teaching, etc., all help to create a rounded character by understanding what she has been exposed to; these experiences color her experience and world view.

The **psychology** of the character is not just the product of the other two categories, although it can be first grasped this way. **Personality development** is far more complex. Numerous theories try to explain it and a study of any of them will help a writer. Certainly, though, appearance and environment play a part in shaping a person. They contribute to forming one's ambition, temperament, attitude, complexes, and so on.

In order for a character's biography to be effective it needs to address not only what motivates the character to behave as he does, but also why he is in the predicament he is in. Without providing a clear understanding of these questions, the biography becomes merely a list of interesting—but not especially helpful— information.

Again, the essential things the writer must know about the protagonist are: What does he want and why, and what does he need emotionally? The **character biography** must lead to the answers to these questions. *The Art of Dramatic Writing* gives an excellent example of this approach.

Backstory

Backstory and **character biography** are not identical but are very similar; both deal with the character's important history. The crucial difference is this: **Backstory** focuses on specific past events that directly affect the protagonist's emotional involvement in the plot as the story unfolds. In a sense, all else is irrelevant. This is what defines the character in the story. This is why he or she is the protagonist in the film. Often it is connected to the protagonist's need. Many writers feel the character's backstory is all they need to know to begin writing. Though a detailed character biography would include this information, these writers don't use one.

In "Life Lessons," the most important piece of Lionel's backstory isn't given fully until the end, though we get hints along the way. This revelation of character is indeed the point of the film. Though Lionel has said he loves Paulette throughout, this is finally cast into doubt when he meets the young and beautiful female painter serving wine at his art opening. Clearly taken with her, he offers her Paulette's job. As we watch their interaction, we sense, correctly, that Lionel is about to start a new version of the cycle he just completed with Paulette. He's incapable of true love with a person, his true love is his canvas.

All the information in the character's **biography** or **backstory** won't necessarily come out in the screenplay. What specifically does come out should provide us with insight about the past that helps us make sense of the character's present. Why is a character afraid to feel or to love? Why is she angry or cynical, bold or cowardly? It's important to remember that these emotions must impinge and push the screenplay one way or another. They must be addressed in the film.

The **backstory** should not get in the way of the current story. Giving too much backstory only weighs down the present situation. What we need to know of backstory is this: How is the character's current behavior related to his past life?

Emotions, Attitudes & Actions

It's not enough just to think about who the character is, where she comes from, and what she wants in order to create a full-blooded characterization. The character can only come alive when she has emotions and attitudes; only the action of the screenplay can illustrate these emotions.

Emotion and the Importance of Identification

The emotional/psychological life of a character is probably the most important aspect of **characterization** (next to want, why and need). Here is where **motivations** are born. Yet it is usually the trait most neglected by beginning, intermediate and even advanced writers. **Emotional reactions** to the story's dramatic events are too often glanced over or totally ignored. Emotions may be expressed by anger or tears, with little range in between. Without emotion, a story is mechanical and contrived; a long shaggy dog story.

True emotion is the source of our connection to other people. We see someone in pain and it elicits feelings of sympathy. We watch people celebrating and their joy makes us smile. Emotion is one of the great universals, connecting human being to human being despite sexual and ethnic differences. Emotion is the basis of the audience's identification with the characters in the film. If we see a mother defending her young, whether she is the Vietnamese woman in *Platoon*, the Anglo prostitute in *Les Miserables*, or the wolf roaming the Canadian wilds in *Never Cry Wolf*, our response will be the same: we root and hope and feel for her. We become involved in her crisis.

Audience **identification** is established if your characters create emotions we recognize at once, such as love, joy, hate, jealousy, fear, humiliation, etc. These are timeless and universal in life. This is why period pieces such as *Lawrence Of Arabia*, *Dances With Wolves* and *Sense And Sensibility* succeed. The characters are recognizable through their emotional responses to the situations and obstacles they face. The reason? We have all encountered some type of unkindness, embarrassment, neglect or cruelty in our lives and we never forget these experiences. The same is true of compassion, generosity and love. They affect us as they affect our characters.

Stories are told in terms of relationships which are matrices of emotions we share with others. If a character pursues a goal and his actions affect no one, he can't affect the audience. He must relate to other characters, positively or negatively, in order to stir and sway the audience. Just as in our lives, relationships on the screen have meaning only to the extent they engage and arouse our emotions. We love or hate, and in drama, these emotions cause us to respond one way or another. (We care or feel disdain for someone and this colors how we react.) Great writers—screenwriters, novelists, playwrights—understand that this is the source of a character's true motivation and find actions which are both logical and surprising to represent the emotion. When their writing succeeds, we call them inspired.

Incorporating a progression of emotions into the plot of the screenplay helps us better understand the character and her motivations. A profound disappointment to a pragmatic might lead to depression and ultimately a spiritual crisis. A show of mercy at the right moment to a miscreant might lead to a painful reassessment of life and a spiritual rebirth. Including emotionally varying scenes increases the depth and complexity of the story as well as helps insure the audience's involvement.

In "Mara Of Rome," we see Mara's (played by Sophia Loren) anger burn deeply when she is scorned by Umberto's grandmother. When her client Rosconi (played by Marcello Mastroianni) arrives, this anger consumes her. She can't deal with him and his lust. Her anger drives him away and he vows never to return. Yet the next day, after she has reconciled with Rosconi and they are finally going to bed, Mara is interrupted by the old woman. Her first reaction is trepidation (after all, the old hag has threatened to get a petition signed against Mara and to throw her out). Mara chains the door and opens it an inch, coolly rebuffing the old woman. But when she sees the old lady break down, Mara melts and invites her nemesis inside, wanting nothing more than to assuage the old woman's pain. It is a marvelous moment which tells everything we need to know about Mara's character.

One emotion that the audience can generally understand, if not identify with, is fear. Many writers believe that the most important element to know about their characters is what they fear. In a sense, if you know what the character is most afraid of, then you know what he needs to face. This is true for the characters populating short films and features. Think of Lionel in "Life Lessons." What does he fear? That Paulette will leave him and he won't be able to paint anything worthwhile; he must keep Paulette around so he can paint. This explains the neurotic way he pursues her, as if everything else in the world counted on her staying. Unconscious fear often drives a character. Robert Towne once said, when he knows what his character fears, he knows he has his character.

Attitudes, Beliefs & Values

Everyone has a **point of view** or **attitude** toward the world. It can be sentimental or cynical, positive or negative, happy or sad. Often a writer first conceives or "gets" the character through attitude, i.e., the hard-boiled cop, the cynical politician. To avoid stereotypes, an insightful writer will show this to be a persona or outward face, and will include another side to the character. Perhaps the hard-boiled cop meticulously cares for his fingers because he plays the violin. The cynical politician may still love the idea of democracy but he no longer believes in it. The key is finding the other side of the person which gives the character complexity.

Attitudes are based mainly on one's beliefs. In film, we don't want to hear a character explain his philosophy. Instead we rely on his attitude and actions to show us what he believes in and values. Everyone believes in something and knowing a character's beliefs brings new dimensions to the story. For example, the overworked secretary: will she fight for women's rights or sit at home and whine about them? The tough longshoreman: will he support his son's pursuit of an education or be threatened by it? In our own lives, too, actions—more than words—tell us who someone is. No matter what people say, a person is truly defined by what he does. A character's beliefs influence his attitude and actions. The stronger the belief, the more definite the attitude and the action.

Values tell us what someone holds dear. Values are important because, along with beliefs, they tell us what a character will or will not fight for. This can be translated into action.

Opinions also help define the character. They let us know what the character thinks about people or the action in the story. If viewers share the character's opinion of what's happening on the screen, it can increase their identification with the character and their involvement in the story.

Attitudes & the Psychological Life

One final note on emotions and attitudes: It is important to understand that, at a deeper level, our emotional and psychological life plays a large part in determining our attitudes and beliefs. Constantin Stanislavski, author of *The Actor Prepares*, said, "First there is the **emotion**, then the thought," and most psychologists would agree. An individual may have specific talents, be predisposed toward extroversion or introversion. She may be naturally inclined to deal with the world through her feeling-based reactions or through intellectually-based efforts to understand. Intuition may be her primary guide or she may be led by her senses. Whatever the case—cynic, optimist, realist, romantic, neurotic—these attitudes are, to an extent, all rooted in the character's past emotional/psychological experiences. Positive interactions with the world produce positive attitudes; negative interactions produce negative ones.

Choices, Commitments & Actions

Drama depends upon action and conflict. In film, character is understood in the context of action, and this is, in fact, most of what we see on the screen. But before someone can take action, a choice must be made. That choice forms the basis of a commitment for the protagonist. It is the decision to commit to something that starts the story.

The best stories are on some level about **choices** and **commitments**. A character determines what he or she wants and decides to pursue it. The story then shows the protagonist's commitment, the **consequences** of taking action, and the **sacrifices** made because of that choice. Choices, commitment and action define the character.

Many short films begin with the protagonist having already made a choice or decision. Lionel is already in love with Paulette at the start of "Life Lessons." He has chosen Paulette but she has not chosen him, and there lies the conflict. Throughout the film, Paulette vacillates between staying in New York or going home, lending hope to

Lionel's quest. But by the end she makes her choice and leaves Lionel and New York.

In "Anna Of Milan" (written by Cesare Zavattini and Billa Billa, directed by Vittorio De Sica and included in *Yesterday, Today And Tomorrow*), Anna (played by Sophia Loren), a married socialite, has made the choice to pursue a young man, ostensibly to begin an affair. But in the light of day, the radical Randall (played by Marcello Mastrioianni), who was ready to fall into her arms the night before, is now not so sure. Anna contradicts everything he is working towards. His sexual attraction for her is strong, but it conflicts with his intellectual dissatisfaction. This is the core conflict of the film and we watch to see which course Randall opts to take and how this decision may change as Anna reacts.

Often, feature and short films glance over the act of deciding, afraid the decision will slow or stop the action. But the process of coming to a **decision** is an action. Seeing someone consider and reflect on what to do can help increase our understanding of that character. We see the weight of the decision. Watching someone rashly push ahead without thinking reveals a different kind of character.

Again, in "Life Lessons," Lionel is not a man who stops and thinks and makes a decision. He doesn't decide. Lionel acts, without thought of the consequences. He will say and do anything in his nearly irrational pursuit of Paulette. This tells us he is a man in love. But by the end of the movie, we have a different picture of what love means to him when he impulsively decides to offer Paulette's job to the aspiring female painter. On the other hand, Paulette can't decide what to do. One moment she is leaving, the next she has allowed Lionel to change her mind. Her indecision defines her. Her actions also help us sympathize with Lionel's frustration dealing with her. Yet as we watch her move from one choice to its opposite, we sense the depth of her conflict and begin to glean its source: she is in the grips of a major identity crisis and Lionel is totally oblivious.

In *The Thoroughbred* (written by Kent Danne and directed by Harold Huth) the protagonist Fitshue decides to go along with the bookie (Kell) when he's able to favor a different horse by placing a bet for Miss Kenneally; this way he can consider himself still morally clean. But when Kell tries to insure his stake in the race by demanding Fitshue drug Miss Kenneally's horse, Fitshue must make a choice. The drama hinges upon this choice and it becomes the defining moment for Fitshue's character.

The **decisions** and **choices** at the beginning and the end of the story are the most important and revealing about the character. The beginning decision is made when the protagonist decides what he wants and commits to pursuing it. In a sense, the film becomes a test of that **commitment** and the price he will pay for maintaining it. Usually—well before the end of most feature films—there is a moment when the protagonist recommits to his goal. In a short film, the choice at the end often leads to the **revelation** of character on which the story is based.

The protagonist's important decision (usually at the end) is best represented to the audience in the form of a choice. The either/or formula makes the choice specific, clarifying to the audience what is at stake for the character. Will he choose the girl and give up an assignment in Rome? The more specific the choice, the easier it is for the audience to grasp. For the choice to convey real meaning, there must be a personal cost for the protagonist.

To deepen the significance of these choices and commitments, examine the cost of your protagonist's decisions and actions to himself and others. The action he takes will be stronger if it costs him something as well as gains him something. In "Mara Of Rome," from *Yesterday, Today And Tomorrow*, Mara vows to sacrifice a week's income if Umberto returns to the seminary. Often, personal loss is expressed in terms of relationship. Lionel loses Paulette essentially because of his commitment to art.

The **decisions** and **choices** the protagonist makes lead to action which then propels the story forward because action produces consequence. This is where character intersects plot; at some point, they should merge and become inseparable. (See Chapter Four: Plotting.)

Audiences judge a character by her actions. So important is action that very often, the audience tends to believe the opposite of what a character says. If he talks tough but acts with kindness, the audience will accept the character's words as a façade and perceive the kindness as his true nature. Such is the power of action for a character in film: People are what they do, not what they say. Actions speak louder than words.

Transformation

In feature films, one of the main characters must noticeably and convincingly be altered by events. This need not always be the protagonist. Sometimes in features, the protagonist is the **agent for change**: Her heroic actions cause other characters to be transformed. This is more often the case in short films, i.e., Mara doesn't change but Rosconi and Umberto do in "Mara Of Rome."

In the best feature films, the protagonist, at some level, undergoes his own transformation. *Witness*, *The Piano*, *Groundhog Day*, *Quiz Show* all are great films in which the protagonist undergoes a profound **transformation** of character. At the end of these films, the hero is at a psychologically healthier position than at the start. The film is, in a sense, a journey which charts the character's transformational arc. Because he meets the conflict, the protagonist is forced to make choices. The result of these choices pushes him to discover qualities within him that compel him to grow. This growth allows him to solve the problem and reach his goal.

At its best, drama examines the costs of the protagonist's actions, usually in terms of personal relationships. Part of the drama comes from what he leaves behind or forsakes in order to gain his goal. In *Witness*, protagonist John Book (played by Harrison Ford) trades his gun for acceptance in the household and this leads to a change in his values. Ada (played by Holly Hunter) in *The Piano* trades her body for her piano and is changed by the experience. In *Quiz Show*, Van Doren (played by Ralph Fiennes) trades his integrity and name for money and notoriety while Stempel (played by John Turturro) exchanges his own notoriety for revenge. These costs are trade-offs; gains come from losses, losses from gains. Audiences ask of these trade-offs: "Were they worth it?"

In a short film, character transformation cannot be as pronounced as in a feature. The same distinction exists between novels and short stories: The former allow heroes a complete reexamination of the human condition; the latter usually detail one incident that offers a challenge to an accepted orthodoxy. In the short film, the protagonist doesn't always change, but his character and actions affect others, and this is the point, as in "Life Lessons," "Mara Of Rome," "Anna Of Milan," and *Peel*.

Sometimes short films effectively chart a progression, as from bad to worse. In the Academy Award-winning short *The Appointments Of Dennis Jennings*, written by Steven Wright and Mike Armstrong, and directed by Dean Parisot, Dennis (played by Steven Wright) the protagonist, is clearly disturbed at the start of the film: He is stalking with a hunting rifle a man in the woods (played by Rowan Atkinson). The story flashes back three months and shows, through a series of very funny encounters Dennis has with an unattentive and unfeeling psychiatrist (his intended victim at the beginning), what drives him to attempt murder. The film climaxes when Dennis shoots his shrink and ends with him in police custody ironically about to be interviewed by a court-appointed psychologist.

Many films show the protagonist becoming aware of some hidden aspect of his or her personality. This coming to consciousness, or recognition of a "new" reality represents real growth for the character. "The Man In The Brooks Brothers Shirt" is a good example of personal growth through the protagonist's interaction with the antagonist.

The short screenplay writer should recognize that the best short films often have an interesting and forceful protagonist who does not change in the course of the story, but forces another major character to change. If you are blocked with your story by an inability to perceive the lesson learned by your protagonist, ask instead what lesson your protagonist could teach another character (and us). Even if your protagonist comes to no new awareness of his lot in life, he should be so compelling that his behavior has given us new insight into ourselves.

Unity of Opposites

The concept of "unity of opposites" is often misunderstood, and so misapplied. Unity of opposites is the unbreakable bond, standing for whatever binds the protagonist and the antagonist (the opposites) together. If the characters are a husband and wife, we might say that love, home, children, etc., unite them. If their natures are completely opposite, then there is bound to be conflict. The story will revolve around that conflict, with the understanding that they are still united by their desire for love, home, children, etc. Each may want dominion over the home and so have opposing, or opposite, agendas. But they are bound in unity to the battlefield spoils of familial supremacy. The resolution can come only when something gives or changes at the climax. We say unity is strong when the protagonist and the antagonist are locked together with no compromise in sight, when the competition is zero-sum in nature, i.e., when one wins, one necessarily loses.

Finding the unity of opposites that keeps the characters in conflict until the climax can be difficult. The best place to look for it is in the motivations of the protagonist and the antagonist. In "Life Lessons," Lionel's motivation to pursue Paulette comes not from his professed love for her but from his need for turmoil in order to paint. Paulette's motivation to stay in New York comes from her desire to be an artist and from her fear of making a wrong decision at this point in her life. In a sense, it is their love of art that unites them. What makes them opposites starts with the polarity between men and women. It continues with his success, talent, and money versus her obscurity and uncertainty—Lionel is at the top of his field while Paulette is unsure if she even has the drive and talent to climb the same artistic ladder.

The more specific manner by which the antagonists are locked together, the better. In *Peel*, the unity consists of the brother/sister relationship. In "Mara Of Rome," Mara is locked into her problem with the grandmother because they are neighbors and share a common wall. Rosconi is bound to Mara because she is the focus of his obsession and the locus of his fantasies; she in turn accepts his money and is obligated to perform various services.

The Important Characters

We've talked a lot about creating and building characters. Although all the characters need loving attention, the ideas and concepts presented above must apply most to your main characters because in all screenplays (but the most obviously melodramatic), it is the main characters who carry the story.

The Protagonist

The most important character in the screenplay is the **protagonist**. He or she is the focus of attention. The protagonist takes the film to the climax. Even in feature films that are considered ensemble pieces, one character usually emerges out of the group as the true protagonist. In a short film, one protagonist carries the storyline. She has the decisions to make and the task to accomplish.

Effective protagonists must appeal to your audience in some way. They do not have to be physically good-looking, but they must have traits or virtues the audience considers admirable or entertaining. The protagonist must be intriguing or sympathetic to keep the audience caring about what happens in the movie. As mentioned above, the protagonist's emotional life and his responses to situations help achieve this.

Attractive traits are generosity, good will, humor, courage, honesty, responsibility or even the consummate skill of a master assassin. Whatever generates respect or admiration holds our interest, at least initially. A protagonist is considered entertaining by his ability to amuse the audience. A character who makes us laugh easily gains our sympathy. A protagonist may have all sorts of **flaws** and weaknesses, but will maintain the audience's sympathy as long as we see he or she is in some manner funny or virtuous. "Life Lessons" Lionel impresses us with his real talent for the canvas, even though we suspect early on that he would be difficult to live with.

A protagonist's qualities must be shown in his action because only actions demonstrate to the audience the character's true self.

Another key aspect of the protagonist's screen personality is commitment to his goal. This commitment leads to conflict which he struggles heroically to overcome on his way towards his goal. Active protagonists grab the audience's interest and hold it. Even an unsympathetic protagonist can keep our attention for awhile if he is struggling valiantly for his goal.

To create a first-rate characterization, the protagonist needs something genuinely unique and something archetypal to separate him from the group. In "Life Lessons," Lionel is an extremely successful artist. Being an artist puts him in a limited group and his success separates him even further, as does his sexual success with a pretty live-in woman. Indeed, Lionel is a particularly rich character because he carries all of the following archetypes: Artistic mentor, spiritual advisor, father-figure, initiator into the sexual world (older man, younger woman), sponsor (he supports Paulette's art), and simple bon vivant.

Finally, contrasting what makes the protagonist unique

against what makes him universal will help bring the characterization to life. Again, using "Life Lessons," what connects Lionel to other people is his unrequited love for Paulette; who hasn't felt unrequited love? We admire the successful artist but identify emotionally with the man losing the girl.

The Antagonist

The **antagonist** is the principal adversary of the hero. He represents the obstacles. The antagonist can be one person or a group of people who oppose the protagonist's pursuit of his goal.

The antagonist does not have to be a "villain" to be effective. In feature films, he is often conceived that way, and the more despicable the better. But in a short film, the antagonist is more often a character standing in the way of the protagonist attaining his goal.

Many successful short films portray the antagonist nearly as fully as the protagonist, exploring her conflict in terms of character and relationship. Paulette, the antagonist in "Life Lessons," is not an evil, remorseless woman. Though flawed, she is struggling with her own problems and this motivates much of her bitchy behavior. At first brush, the grandmother in "Mara Of Rome" is a vicious old hag, but as the conflict develops, a softer side emerges.

The best antagonists are considered as fully as the protagonist. This is generally the primary relationship explored in a short film. Giving the same amount of thought to this character's **wants**, **motivations** (conscious and unconscious), and **needs** in opposition to the protagonist's will help strengthen the overall conflict and story. The more believably drawn the antagonist's wants and needs are, the better he will play against the protagonist.

The antagonist needs to be committed to his goal, too. This commitment should be as strong as the protagonist's to provide the opportunity to maximize conflict between them. Like the protagonist, the antagonist needs to be drawn with emotions and attitudes and given actions to represent them. In addition, understanding what is unique as well as archetypal and universal about the character will help the audience understand him and perhaps empathize with his problem. The grandmother in "Mara Of Rome," though thoroughly disagreeable when we meet her, is understandable in her attitude toward Mara. When she swings from being an adversary to ally, she moves from being the archetypal wicked witch to a fairy godmother in relationship to Mara.

The antagonist is the best way to explore the protagonist, to reveal who that character is. What would we know about Lionel without Paulette for him to obsess upon in "Life Lessons"? What would we know about Tim without Katie in *Peel*? If you try to see this opposing force as fully as the protagonist, then she can emerge as a full character in her own right, instead of being a cardboard cutout moved around solely for plot reasons.

Supporting Characters

A **catalyst** is the character who causes something to happen that involves the protagonist in the conflict which becomes the plot. In "Life Lessons," Paulette becomes the catalyst once she declares she is leaving. In "Mara Of Rome," Umberto is the unwitting catalyst who causes the conflict between Mara and his grandmother. Often in a short film, the catalyst and the antagonist are the same character.

The **confidant** is a close friend of the protagonist. He allows the protagonist to reveal sides of his nature that are not apparent on the surface. Protagonists act differently with confidants than they would with other characters.

Confidants permit the protagonist to show vulnerability, doubt, emotion. But when confidants are used for expository purposes, they tend to slow the story down. In "Life Lessons," Lionel's art dealer Philip Fowler fulfills this role. In the segment entitled "The Gambler" from *The Gold Of Naples* (written by Cesare Zavattini and directed by

Vittorio De Sica), the butler fulfills the role of confidant for the Count.

Exercises

The obvious place to start building a character is by writing a character biography of one or two of your main characters. But before you try this, look at another film and analyze the main characters. Determine what you know about one or more of the characters from what you see in the film. Start with their goals, what they want and what they need. Then, using what the character says about himself, figure out what he does, what others say about him, and ascertain who the character really is. Are there hints about a deeper background for the characters that never really come into play? Is there information given that fills in the details of a life that makes it feel true?

Now, look at your own characters. Consider one and figure out how she became this way. You probably already have an idea of what your character wants. Why she wants it and her need still may be unfocused, so ask about her psychological makeup. Where was she born and how did she grow up? What kind of person is she today? All of this information is especially relevant if it is leads to explaining why the character is in her present predicament.

Now focus on:
1. What does the character **want** (in this story)?
2. **Why** does the character want it?
3. What does the character **need**?

Remember what he *wants* will be stronger if it is something specific, something the audience can easily understand and relate to. *Why* gives us his conscious motivation for wanting it. The *need* tells what the unconscious wants from the character; this often is the true motivation for him. Sometimes it is what the character needs to learn in order to succeed.

To fill out your character, determine which emotions generally rule her life. Is she someone who is in touch with her emotions in a healthy way or is she unable to deal with them? Consider her anxieties; how does she handle them? Does she deny, suppress, escape, or face and assimilate them? Ask what she's afraid of.

What is the character's attitude towards life? Does he think it's a good deal or a bad one? What do his beliefs and values tell you about him?

Another good question is, what does your character want most out of life? This is not the want/plot goal of your film, but a question which, when answered truthfully, defines whoever answers it. Is she consciously pursuing this long-term goal or unconsciously undermining it because of self-destructive patterns within her personality?

These are only a few questions which can provide insight into your characters. Ask the questions of your characters which interest you about people and the answers should provide you with ample information to build a story. Keep these answers handy and consult them often. As you do, you may find the answers changing. That's okay. It should signify you are getting closer to the real truth about your character.

3

THE
THREE-PART NATURE
OF FILM STRUCTURE

"A script is more architecture than literature," Eli Kazan writes in his autobiography *A Life*. The architecture of a film story, whether a feature or a short, generally follows certain basic rules. The beginning of a film must set up the **dramatic problem**. The middle consists of the story's rising action which builds to the final **climax** and **resolution**. This formula is simple enough in theory, but in practice, keeping the characters on track, the story moving ahead, and the audience from becoming bored can be an infuriatingly difficult task.

In this chapter, we lay a foundation for all screenwriting **structure** while giving special attention to the short film. The tools and materials are the same, only the magnitude and scope of the ideas and execution are different. Screenplays, short or long, are all structure, structure, structure.

The Setup

In a short film, the **setup** is much the same as in a feature film. Its goal is to orient the audience to the backdrop, time frame, and mood, and to give the audience a clue as to the direction of the film. It provides the important information the audience needs in order to get the story moving. But instead of taking ten to fifteen pages (minutes) to set the story's tone, characters and action, the short film must accomplish this almost immediately.

The Protagonist & the Main Conflict

The setup introduces the protagonist and his problem: the main conflict of the story. As in a feature, the hero has something he wants and something he needs. The "want" becomes his goal, what he must accomplish. The "need" is usually connected to the reason why he is on this path; it is the true motivation of the story. With good, sharp drama, this need conflicts with what the hero's "wants."

In "Life Lessons," Lionel, the protagonist, says he loves Paulette and wants her to stay. This is clearly his paramount "want." But what he "needs" is for her to cause conflict, to enrage, frustrate and humiliate him because only when he has her in his life, denying him her favors, can he paint. As discussed in Chapter Two, Paulette gives rise to the passion that fuels his painting. She is only the foreplay; art is the climax of Lionel's creative drive.

The Main Exposition

The screenwriter must determine what is primary and vital for the audience to know about the hero and the problem that cannot unfold through dramatic action. This information, the **main exposition**, must be communicated at the story's start, often through dialogue, to convey to the audience what it needs to know in relation to the character and situational background. This important information helps orient the audience to what possibly could happen in the story. Generally, this introductory exposition requires more than one scene.

In "Life Lessons" we see immediately that Lionel Dobie is a successful artist. We know he is an artist by his paints, brushes, canvases and studio. The expensive cognac he drinks while he tries to paint tells us he is successful, as does the enormous studio and megawatt boom box. His paint-coated fingers and the manic look in his eyes tell us he's totally dedicated to his craft. All this is shown under the film's opening credits.

The first scene introduces Lionel's art dealer, Philip, who comes to the studio to see the artist's new work; Lionel has three weeks until a big exhibition. But Lionel will not show Philip's work. He's nervous, scared, depressed. "I'm going to get slaughtered," he groans. When Philip suggests lunch, Lionel tells him he has to pick up his assistant at the airport. This scene, primarily all exposition, establishes the possible story problem (the art show) and drives the story to a second piece of exposition in the following scene.

In a short screenplay, every word, every line must advance the action and reveal only what is necessary to understand the characters and the story. There is no time for incidental information. Every word must be to the point, especially at the beginning. Other insights and information about the hero or other characters can be revealed as the story advances, and as the audience needs it in order to comprehend the progressive actions of the hero.

The Inciting Incident

The setup of the film is complete once the **inciting incident** starts the story in motion. The inciting incident is like a **catalyst**, it forces the main conflict out into the open and demands that the hero act. The inciting incident gets the hero on his path in pursuit of his goal. This action concludes the main exposition.

The second scene in "Life Lessons" is the film's catalyst. At the airport, Lionel waits anxiously for his assistant Paulette. Everything is in slow motion to emphasize both his impatience and his total concentration on her. When she gets off the plane, what he lives for has arrived. He absentmindedly crushes his cigarette into the carpeted floor. Paulette is upset, too, because he's there. She didn't want to see him. She tells him she's leaving New York. He is incredulous and tries to convince her to stay.

The setup is complete. The main conflict is established: Lionel declares his love for Paulette and spends the rest of the film trying to convince her to stay. Painting becomes his refuge after each of Paulette's rebuffs. On the surface, his unrequited love seems to be the reason he couldn't paint at the beginning. But as the story unfolds, we see that the author's intent (and Lionel's unconscious need) is exactly the opposite.

The structure of the setup doesn't have to follow the order of these events. The inciting incident can come before the protagonist is introduced and the main exposition given.

The Italian film *Especially On Sunday*, written by Tonino Guerra, contains three shorts. The first segment, "The Blue Dog," directed by Giuseppe Tornatore, establishes Amleto (played by Philippe Noiret) as a shoemaker, in several quick shots, without showing his face. A dog with a splotch of blue paint between the eyes pokes its head in the front door and suddenly the shoemaker hurls the heel of a shoe at it. The heel misses the dog, flies into the street and hits a midget, raising all kinds of protest. In the following scene, we meet Amleto and his background is laid out in expository dialogue. We learn he is a bachelor and ask, along with the townspeople, why he hates the dog?

In Jane Campion's short *Peel*, the **main exposition** is given in the form of cards indicating the relationships between the main characters before we even meet them.

The Problem & the Subproblem

A film needs a **main problem** that is dramatic and has consequences for the protagonist. Identifying the problem often is helpful for outlining purposes and to pose the problem in the form of a question. In "Life Lessons," the dramatic question is: Will Lionel convince Paulette to stay? In the short *The Thoroughbred*: Will Fitshue help the bookie Kell fix the race? In "Mara Of Rome": Will Mara assuage the grandmother and get Umberto to return to the seminary?

Many short films raise more than one question. Secondary questions may be considered **subproblems**. Subproblems may concern the protagonist, antagonist, or another character who indirectly affects the protagonist. They are conflicts of secondary importance which impact the plot. In concept, they resemble **subplots** in feature length films. Both subplots and subproblems commence secondary storylines which are dramatized in the construction of the plot. Both are used to give dimension to a story and often carry the theme. But where a subplot in a feature always begins after the introduction of the main conflict and ends before the main climax, a subproblem in a short film can start before the main conflict and end in the resolution. Used this way, a **subproblem** frames the main problem for the protagonist. This technique allows the audience an alternate view of the conflict by providing a last insight into the main character or story. A **subproblem** for the antagonist begins with the opposing character's introduction, and generally ends in the climax.

Using "Life Lessons" again, the **subproblem** for Lionel is: Will he complete his paintings before his exhibition and how will the show turn out? The story also raises a subproblem for Paulette: Will she leave New York? *The Thoroughbred* asks if Miss Kenneally's horse will win the race. In "Mara Of Rome": Will Rosconi ever make love with Mara?

The specific **subproblem** raises another question in the viewer's mind which must be answered by the end of the screenplay. If it is not resolved, the audience is less likely to feel the film has a true resolution.

Raising more than one issue in the mind of the viewer increases the chances of greater involvement in the film. Seeking more than a single answer to a setup means we need to hear a story, not a series of yes/no responses. The more complicated your setup, the more questions it raises, the more compelling your story.

If you are working within the confines of a thirty-page screenplay, the **setup** must be conveyed in the first five pages. If your movie is ten minutes (i.e., a screenplay length of ten to twelve pages), you must establish your main conflict through the **main exposition** and **inciting incident** by the first or second page. The goal is to set your story in motion as quickly as possible.

The Rising Action

Once the **setup** is complete, the main action begins. In dramatic terms, this is called the rising action. The protagonist has expressed her want; the goal is clear. The ensuing action is what the protagonist does to achieve his goal. The conflict is what stands in her way.

The Antagonist

The **antagonist** best represents this conflict. Though a story can exist with only a psychic or internal conflict, a specific antagonist lends clarity and power to the dramatic structure because her primary function is to oppose the protagonist. She is not necessarily evil, but rather personifies the protagonist's obstacles. Frequently, the antagonist initiates the protagonist's (and the drama's) crucial problem. In psychological terms, the antagonist may represent those everyday forces that keep heroes sitting behind desks in jobs they hate instead of out fighting their battles. In a sense, the antagonist represents a real break for the protagonist; at least the hero will fight due to the antagonist's presence. Keep this in mind when thinking about motivating your protagonist: What will get him to put on his gloves and fight? What will get her mad enough to draw the line in the sand?

In "Life Lessons," Paulette is the antagonist. Her wish to leave New York directly conflicts with Lionel's desire for her to stay. In "Anna Of Milan" Randall opposes Anna. In *The Thoroughbred*, Kell, the bookie and blackmailer trying to fix the race, is the antagonist.

The Plan

The protagonist usually has a **plan** he starts carrying out once his problem has been introduced. It may be conscious or instinctive, carefully thought-out or arbitrary. The plan often finds its way into the protagonist's dialogue soon after the action begins so the audience will know his intention. The plan also allows the audience to grasp how the protagonist initially sees the conflict and anticipates the results. As the story progresses, the gap between the protagonist's expected results and reality (the main conflict) should produce story surprise and lead to greater struggle. As the protagonist perseveres, he reveals his true character and the audience gains insight into the meaning of the story.

In "Life Lessons," Lionel's plan is arbitrary. He will plead, promise, lie, cajole, scare, threaten, or do anything to convince Paulette to stay. In "Mara Of Rome," Mara makes a sacred vow and promises to help the grandmother convince Umberto to return to the seminary.

Rising action, by definition, requires a variety of escalating conflicts confronting the protagonist to keep the story interesting. If the conflict is not varied, stories seem repetitive. Below are some specific story tools that may be useful for the construction of a plot.

Obstacles

The clearest form of conflict is an **obstacle**. This is something that opposes the protagonist as he attempts to achieve his goal. The best obstacles incite the most action from the characters. Once an obstacle becomes apparent, it should directly threaten at the protagonist.

There are roughly four kinds of **obstacles**:
1. The antagonist
2. Physical obstructions
3. Inner/psychological obstacles
4. Mystic forces.

The **antagonist** already has been mentioned. Physical obstructions are just what they seem: river crossings, desert journeys, mountain climbs, urban jungles and wars. The gallows, river and civil war in the Academy Award Winning short film *Occurrence At Owl Creek* (written and directed by Robert Enrico from a short story by Ambrose Bierce) are good examples of physical obstacles confronting the protagonist.

Inner obstacles are intellectual, emotional or psychological problems the protagonist must overcome before being able to achieve his goal. Fear, pride, jealousy fall into this category. Lionel's jealousy in "Life Lessons" is an inner obstacle he needs to confront in his relationship with Paulette. In Douglas Kunin's short film *Twist Of Fate,* the schizophrenic protagonist faces his numerous inner voices.

Mystic forces enter most stories as **accidents** or **chance**, but they also can be expressed as **moral choices** or **ethical codes** which cause obstacles. They also can be personified as gods or supernatural forces with which the characters must contend. In *Lawrence Of Arabia*, Lawrence must be true to his own inner code which conflicts with the British position on the Arabs. In *Ghost* the protagonist must deal with a paranormal world to in order to reach his lover.

Obstacles are important because when properly conceived and presented, they force the major characters to make decisions. Such decisions produce dramatic action. Dramatic action creates compelling stories.

Complications

Complications are factors that enter the world of the film and cause a change in the action. They differ from **obstacles** in that they don't immediately pose an apparent threat. A complication generally arises during the story and complicates matters for the protagonist. They work best when they are unexpected. Complications also add tension through anticipation because the audience must wait for the hero's inevitable reaction. Typically, they can arrive in the form of a character or they can be a circumstance, event, mistake, misunderstanding or discovery. Complications also can develop specific characteristics about the protagonist (or antagonist), as well as elucidate the story's theme.

In *The Thoroughbred*, Miss Kenneally's prevailing upon Fitshue to train her horse Minstrel is the story's complication. Fitshue knows Minstrel does not have a chance of winning, but the woman shames him into helping her. This later contributes to his problem with Kell. In "Mara Of Rome," Umberto is the complication that leads to the conflict Mara has with both the grandmother and her client Rosconi.

Again, **obstacles** arise once (unless it is the antagonist who recurs) and are immediate impediments to the hero's story goal. **Complications** undulate through a story, arising at different points to engage the hero — less as an obstacle to overcome and more as a lingering character or circumstance that will deepen our understanding of the hero's view of the world.

The Reversal

A **reversal** is one of the strongest tools a writer can use in a film. It changes the direction of the story one hundred and eighty degrees and obviously causes new developments. It must surprise the audience, working physically or emotionally to reverse the action or a character's emotions.

In *The Thoroughbred*, Fitshue repeatedly refuses to help Kell divert the odds from the favorite horse in the race. Kell finally blackmails Fitshue into agreeing, however, and Fitshue must reverse himself. In "Life Lessons," by the time Paulette returns to the studio from the airport, Lionel seems to have convinced her that New York is the place to be if she wants to be an artist. She makes him promise that she won't have to sleep with him anymore. "I'm your ally against horse dung and fraud," he tells her, as he agrees to be a platonic mentor from now on. But even though Lionel is obsessed with Paulette, he still can't tell her what she longs to hear about her art work. He critiques her paintings with words like "nice" and "little," avoiding what she really wants to know: Is she any good? Does she have any talent? Will she ever be good? "You're young yet," Lionel says, and this upsets her. He then responds by saying that art is about having to do it, not about what other people think. This frustrates her all the more. She calls home to ask if she can return for awhile, then goes to tell Lionel she's leaving. Ensphered in blasting music, Lionel paints, oblivious to her cries and all else in his secular world. As she watches him, Paulette's anger melts. This is why she came to New York: Lionel painting represents all that she loves about art. Here, she weakens and reverses herself, deciding to stay.

Crisis

A **crisis** occurs whenever the hero confronts an **obstacle**. It creates conflict in the action because the outcome of a crisis is always in doubt. The action may be an attempt to reach a goal or capture a stake, but since there is an obstruction, the hero cannot prevail at the moment. The screenwriter dramatizes the action in a **crisis** to demonstrate the protagonist's commitment to his goal. Because the outcome remains uncertain until the end, crises arouse suspense. They also necessitate decisions. The protagonist and antagonist must decide whether or not to struggle, and if so, how that struggle will occur. Crises involve some combination of physical, verbal, emotional and, intellectual activity on the part of one or more of the characters. Crises build crises and these escalate and intensify the action until the climax is reached.

"Life Lessons" is full of crises because Lionel and Paulette are in constant conflict. The first crisis arises when Paulette announces she is leaving and Lionel clearly wants her to stay. The next crisis is Paulette's personal one: After Lionel critiques her work and shakes what little confidence she had, she calls her mom and asks about coming home. This crisis is more muted, but difficult just the same.

How many of these story tools you employ depends upon the length of your film. If you expect a running time of ten minutes, one complication impeding the progress of the protagonist could create enough conflict to hold the audience's interest. If your film is longer, then it would be wise to employ a combination of obstacles, complications, reversals and crises. The real secret as to what, how many, and when these tools are used is provided by your characters. Their decisions and actions should move the plot.

The Midpoint

The period of rising action is usually the longest segment of the film, corresponding to the second act of a play or feature. To make this section easier to manage, you may want to break it down into two halves. The **midpoint** takes us to a surprise, a reversal or a new complication in the story. The dramatic problem might even appear solved— for the moment. In "Life Lessons," Paulette's reversal and her decision to stay is the midpoint. As she reconsiders her decision to leave New York, Paulette tells us something about herself: it is Lionel's art, not the man, that keeps her. Can that be enough to hold her to him? This question leaves the climax in doubt.

In "The Blue Dog" from *Especially On Sunday*, the **midpoint** occurs when someone else shoots the persistent dog. Even though that had been Amleto's intent, he is stunned and then upset. The next morning, he follows a trail of blood to find out what has happened to the dog.

In *The Thoroughbred*, Kell's blackmailing of Fitshue convinces him to reverse himself. This is the midpoint and, because it is unexpected, it forces the story to take a new direction. This leads to the second section of rising action. At this point, the action builds again, this time to a final crisis, climax and resolution.

In "Mara Of Rome," the grandmother comes to Mara's house and asks for her help in stopping Umberto from leaving the seminary. Before this scene, the two women are enemies. By the time the scene is over, they are friends.

The Main Crisis

In order to reach the climax, the conflict must intensify and increase, causing the action to rise for the last time. The struggle between the protagonist and the antagonist comes out into the open. Now there must be a definite solution to the problem.

After the **midpoint** in "Life Lessons," the conflict heats up again. Let's look at it.

Unable to control his jealousy, Lionel embarrasses Paulette at a tony New York art party when another man shows interest in her. (Young men are Lionel's complications with Paulette, as they reveal his jealousy and insecurity.) To get even, she brings the man back to the studio and sleeps with him there, escalating the conflict. The audience wonders what Lionel will do. He paints with a vengeance.

Next, Lionel apologizes and gives Paulette advice on how to handle the performance artist, Gregory Stark, who dumped her at the beginning of the film. When she tries to retreat from her proposed plan and remain in New York to paint, Lionel admonishes her not to use her painting as an escape. "Your work is sacred," he says. So Lionel accompanies Paulette to see Stark's new piece at a club; she will congratulate him and show him there are no hard feelings. She barely gets out a "hi" before other people interrupt and distract him. This makes her feel worse and causes another crisis for Paulette. Lionel, trying to comfort her, declares his love again. But she blames him for making her feel foolish and insignificant. She dares him to kiss a policeman to prove his love for her and then ditches him. Now he's the one who feels foolish.

Returning to his studio, Lionel finds Paulette making tea. Barely clad in a robe, she is clearly teasing him. The conflict takes a dark turn: Lionel threatens her. He could rape her or murder her. He could do anything because, "I'm nothing to you," he says. She only smiles, sphinx-like, and goes off to bed. Lionel throws himself back at his canvas.

The last straw comes when Paulette meets a girlfriend for a drink, coincidentally, in the same restaurant as Lionel and his art dealer. Who should present himself but Stark, the performance artist. He invites her to see his new show, the one she just saw. Lionel breaks in before she can respond and tells him off, embarrassing her again. She exits and Lionel punches Stark.

All of these incidents between the two characters dramatize their conflict. The scenes build to a breaking point, which takes us to the climax of the film.

The **setup** requires approximately one to five pages in a thirty-page screenplay, so you should allot twenty to twenty-five pages for the **rising action**. Thus, the two halves of the rising action on either side of the **midpoint** might be around ten to fifteen pages each.

The Climax & Resolution

The **climax** is the highest, most exciting point in the drama, during which the conflict must finally be resolved, one way or the other. The climax involves a discovery or realization for the characters, or at least for the audience. In film, the best climax is visual and emotional, not internal. It can be one scene or it can unfold over the course of several.

In "Life Lessons," Lionel finds Paulette back at the studio. She is angrily knocking over her paintings. Apologetic yet again, he tries to stop her. "Don't do that," he says. "Are you trying to punish me?"

"Am I punishing you?" she incredulously responds. He entirely misses the point: her actions are directed at herself. They have it out. Frustration with her art and herself is what fuels her crisis. His needs, demands, self-absorption are all secondary. "Am I good? Will I ever be any good?" she wants to know. And Lionel can't tell her. He confesses he is the problem; he indulges himself, his passion, his art. He melodramatically offers to give up painting for her and become a "nice person," asking pointedly if that's what she wants. This is the breaking point. Paulette screams she doesn't care what he does. She can't take it anymore. She's going home, and must threaten, physically drive him from her room.

In the next scene, Paulette comes in to say good-bye. Her brother has arrived to help her move out. She again watches Lionel paint, still clearly awed by it. If only he had told her once, she says, that she was a terrible painter and should get a job, she might have believed he really cared for her. Lionel angrily spins from his work. "You think I just use people," he says. "Well, you don't know anything about me. You don't know how involved I get or how far down I go. Hell, I was married four times since before you were born, so don't you tell me."

Paulette backs away and leaves as Lionel angrily returns to his painting. He mumbles to himself about chippies. "You know why they call 'em that?" he asks himself. "Because they like to chip away at you, man. Take a little chip at your art form, at your talent. Chip, chip, chip." And then suddenly he realizes what he's said. More than anything else before, this reveals his feelings for Paulette and women in general.

The Resolution

At the end of the film is the **resolution**, the falling action. The problems not resolved in the climax are taken care of here. This final part of the structure realigns the parameters of the screenplay's world as a result of the climax, fixing the fates of the main characters involved in the struggle, especially those the audience might be most interested in. The best resolution bestows a final insight or **revelation** on the story which puts everything into context by elucidating the **theme** (more on this in Chapter Seven). All of this happens in the last couple of pages. In a very short film, the resolution need be only one scene, or part of one. More often than not, the resolution in a short film is included in the climax.

"Life Lessons" ends at Lionel's exhibition. It's clearly an event and his paintings are a big success. Even he is impressed and satisfied with the work. As he admires one of his paintings, he gets a glass of wine at the bar. A lovely young artist touches his arm for luck. As it turns out she is struggling to make ends meet. Smitten, he winds up offering her Paulette's job. In this final moment, the audience learns the whole affair with Paulette was "nothing personal" and Lionel is into the cycle again.

Exercises

View a short film. Look at the structural considerations first.

1. Identify the underlying concept, the story idea and the dramatic problem.
   a. Who is the protagonist?
   b. What does he or she want?
   c. How is this established?
   d. Where does conflict stem from?
   e. What is the inciting incident?
   f. How long does it take for the problem to surface?
   g. Does the protagonist's need come into play in defining the conflict?

2. Is there a subproblem for one of the main characters?
   a. If so, how is it used?
      1. To frame the main conflict?
      2. To fill in other characters?

3. Does there seem to be an escalation in the main conflict?
   a. What are the main obstacles the protagonist encounters?
   b. Are there external and internal obstacles for the protagonist?
   c. Do the complications impact the protagonist in a positive or negative way?
   d. Is there a distinct midpoint to the plot?

1. What happens there?
2. How does the action change or develop as a result of what happens?
3. Is it a reversal?

4. Is there a main crisis?
   a. Is it fully realized in terms of the screenplay's basic conflict?
   b. Is the film's dramatic problem crystalized in the main crisis?

5. Does the main crisis lead to the climax?
   a. Is it the strongest emotional experience?
   b. Does the climax solve the film's dramatic problem?
      1. What happens to the protagonist as a result?
      2. Does he change?
      3. Does someone else change?
   d. Does the climax sum up the meaning of the film?

6. Is the resolution a result of the basic conflict?
   a. Is it purposeful?
   b. Does it make a commentary on the problem?
   c. What is the commentary?

7. Finally, what is the film's theme?
   a. Has it been motivated by the central idea?
   b. Is it valid, true?
   c. Is this theme implicitly or explicitly stated?
   d. If it is implicit, how do we know it?

4

PLOTTING— THE TWISTS & TURNS

Constructing a believable, exciting plot is never easy. You must know who the protagonist is, what she wants, and who or what opposes her. (The more you know about the protagonist and what she wants, the easier the problem of plot will be to solve.) You need to have a general idea of the story. Good plot grows out of decisions the protagonist makes and actions she takes as a result; the same is true of the antagonist. (Everything you know about the antagonist helps your understanding of the obstacles presented to the protagonist.) It is paramount to know your characters, what they stand for and what they don't, to know what they will do when confronted with a particular situation. Similarly, thinking out the story will help make developing the plot a less difficult task.

In the last chapter, we discussed the overall structure of a short film and illustrated various forms of conflict the protagonist can face. Now we focus on the process of selecting and ordering the scenes that develop the conflict and create the plot—the blueprint for the drama.

Story & Plot

How many times has a friend told you he has a great idea for a film. You sit down and listen to him as he describes his idea in three or four sentences. He's probably giving you the rudiments of a story, but he's far from constructing a plot. As a writer, that's your job.

Story and plot are not synonymous, but they are intimately related. Story, as defined in the *Concise Dictionary of Literary Terms*, is a **sequence of events**, either true or fictitious, designed to interest, amuse or inform hearers, readers, or in our case, viewers. Plot refers to the **arrangement of events** to achieve an intended effect. A plot is a series of carefully devised and interrelated actions which progresses through a struggle of opposing forces to a climax and resolution. It is the form of the work; story is but one kind of plot. E.M. Forster made the distinction between plot and story clear in *Aspects of the Novel*:

> We have defined a story as a narrative of events arranged in their time sequence. A plot is also a narrative of events, the emphasis falling on a causality. "The king died and then the queen died" is a story. "The king died, and then the queen died of grief" is a plot. The time sequence is preserved, but the sense of causality overshadows it.

A story tells a sequential action. A plot emphasizes the causal relationship between actions in a story.

Plot organizes the narrative line around a rising action. The effective use of such factors as conflict, suffering, discovery, reversal, tension, suspense, etc., in the overall arrangement of the plot builds momentum and arouses curiosity. A strong plot appears to be going somewhere. Films which don't have a clear plot often feel aimless; they are merely a sequence of events which do not lead anywhere. Story is the starting point, but the goal in any story is the creation of a plot made of scenes with strong cause-and-effect relationships.

Story and **plot** usually comprise part of a total **narrative**. The narrative consists of all the situations and events pertinent to the film, and includes many that are not actually shown on the screen. All the events previous to the beginning of the film, plus those enacted during the film, make up the narrative. Only the sequential events during the screenplay's time span form the story. The total narrative of "Life Lessons," for example, begins with Lionel's and Paulette's relationship previous to the announcement of his latest show and ends at the close of the film. The following illustration represents the difference between narrative and story:

A_____B_____C

"A" is the beginning of the narrative; it might be considered the backstory. The important events in the narrative leading up to the opening enter the film only as exposition. "B" is the start of the story and the opening of the film. "C" is the ending of the narrative, story, and film.

In "Mara Of Rome," the narrative begins when Mara rents the apartment across the patio from the grandmother and the old lady witnesses the trail of men in and out of Mara's home. This forms part of the backstory of the tale and motivates the old woman's resentment toward Mara. But the screen story begins with the introduction of Umberto into the environment and the problem this sets up between the two women.

In *Peel*, the narrative originates with the conflict between brother and sister, dating back to the dawn of their sibling rivalry.

The Role of Conflict

Action in drama and fiction depends upon **conflict**, which is the starting point of all drama. It is the opposition of persons or forces, the struggle in a plot which grows out of the interaction of opposing ideas, interests or wills. A plot cannot be constructed without conflict.

Plotting, the selection and arrangement of scenes, is really the orchestration of the characters' wants and needs as they move through the story. As your characters attempt to reach their goals, they conflict with each other. The end nears as the protagonist and antagonist approach their goals and the conflict rises to generate maximum suspense and excitement. In order for the conflict to rise, the protagonist and antagonist must be locked together with no compromise possible between them. This is achieved by having characters of strong conviction and purpose, who will fight for what they want. The more evenly matched they are, the stronger the battle will be and the more suspense will be aroused.

If the **unity of opposites** is strong between the characters, the conflict will be strong and so will the plot. Unity can be achieved by characters having the same goal—that only one may win. Family relationships can keep conflicting characters in constant association. Love can bring opposites together. Try to make the unity as specific as possible to understand what is fueling the conflict and what must give in the characters in order to find a resolution.

If the conflict of your story revolves around a situation, or the antagonist is a force and not a person, find a way to personalize the obstacle for the protagonist. A clash of man against nature can be translated into a personal conflict only if the audience understands that nature presents or objectifies a challenge which the protagonist has set for himself. The best way to do this is to find what the force represents to the character. It is not a conflict between man and nature or man and beast, but a struggle going on within the man himself.

In the feature film *The Old Man And The Sea*, adapted from the Ernest Hemingway story by Peter Viertel, the old man is striking back at the encroachments of age, and catching the fish is the only way he can. In another feature film *The Macomber Affair* (again adapted from Hemingway story by Casey Robinson and Seymour Bennett), Macomber is fighting fear—his own—and not a lion. In these stories, and the films made from them, both men are fighting weaknesses within themselves. The fish and lion are ingenious dramatic devices for telling the story in terms of action.

Conflict in a film does not always mean there must be physical violence. Audiences often relate far more quickly to emotional conflict than to physical violence because we have all experienced emotional friction in our own lives; very few adults have escaped life with no emotional scars. In "Hills Like White Elephants," adapted by Joan Didion and John Gregory Dunne and directed by Tony Richardson, from yet another Hemingway story, the emotional conflict escalates to a heart-wrenching recognition for the two protagonists that is sure to be the source of pain for both of them for a long time to come, yet nothing physically untoward occurs in the film.

Physical violence often makes for good drama because it represents the meeting of uncompromising positions. Film will always rely on violence to tell many stories, just as dreams (even for the unproductive dreamer) often use violence to get attention and illustrate their messages. In many successful feature films, and in some of our examples (*Occurrence At Owl Creek*, *The Red Balloon*, *The Appointments Of Dennis Jennings*), physical violence is an intricate part of the story and its success. However, it is more important in a short film for the violence to have a point. Because there is so little time, violence that does not directly serve the story appears all the more gratuitous.

Of course, conflict does not have to be either physically or emotionally violent to illustrate a successful story. "Life Lessons" and "The Man In The Brooks Brothers Shirt" are examples of stories loaded with subtle conflict between the characters: they are not violent but emotional conflicts.

To be effective in constructing a plot, conflict needs to rise in waves. Along the way there are temporary cease-fires or "fixes," but they can't last. "Life Lessons" careens from one temporary solution to another. The first crisis arises when Paulette announces she's leaving and Lionel, clearly, doesn't want her to go. Lionel solves his problem by convincing Paulette to stay after swearing she won't have to sleep with him anymore. This seems to hold until Lionel critiques her work but won't tell her how he really feels about it. This sends Paulette reeling and it looks as though she's headed for home. But she gets caught up in watching him paint and this act reaffirms her commitment to art.

These **short-term solutions** prolong the audience's arrival at the moment of final confrontation with the antagonist. Delaying the confrontation can build tension, but it also allows the writer to fill in important details about the main characters. These details help to affect the audience's relationship to the characters. A plot deepens and grows by including scenes which dramatize the main characters' reactions to the action of the plot. As with real relationships in life, we need time to understand the allies we have and the foes we face.

When the conflict is properly conceived and handled, the drama has a better chance of fulfilling the audience's expectations. Not because viewers are able to predict the outcome, but because the inevitability of the conclusion feels true to them. At the beginning of a screenplay, anything is possible. But after the first scene, the possibilities of what can happen become increasingly limited. Once the beginning indicates a specific situation, group of characters and conflict, the screenwriter leaves the realm of the possible and enters the realm of the probable. The characters must follow one or more lines of **probability** in reaction to the conflict as the plot unfolds so that, by the end, the screenwriter is limited to only what is necessary. Because the characters have said and done specific things, there can be only one necessary resolution.

This doesn't mean the climax is inevitable from the start. The good screenwriter constructs a plot to get the audience asking what will happen next and wondering what the final outcome will be. The plot of a film must appear as though it is changing directions to keep the audience guessing about what may happen. Otherwise, the audience loses interest. (How many times have you heard "predictable" as a put-down of a movie?)

As the protagonist faces **obstacles** and **complications**, his course must alter. New characters bring new possibilities to the plot. Psychological transformations can alter the action. Missed opportunities, misunderstandings, and failures can cast doubt on the story's outcome. Some of the best surprises in films come from the transformation of character. A character changes or grows to do something right or to do something wrong, and in so doing, affects the outcome of the film. It is the screenwriter's job to incorporate and orchestrate these changes into the plot of the film in order for the audience to accept them.

Problems with the ending of a screenplay do not indicate trouble with one or two final scenes, but that a plot has disintegrated—and characters not logically realized—far before that. Audiences often leave a theater saying they like a film but didn't like the ending. As a screenwriter, you must know there are problems long before the end. And, if so, they will manifest themselves in the unsatisfactory finale.

The Principles of Action

Drama is structured action, and structure in drama is crucial. Arbitrary form in a screenplay is deadly. Proper conception and arrangement of scenes engages the audience's interest and curiosity in a character and situation. Good structure carries the momentum of the plot forward, keeping the audience involved in the story.

Plot is not a complex structure created from thin air and then handed over to a group of characters to act out. Plot develops as you turn the general theme and characters into specific details—actions, dialogue, circumstances, time and place. Good plot evolves naturally from the reaction of a particular character in a situation.

In Chapter Two, we spoke of the need for characters who desperately want something and actively pursue their goal. The plot of your story depends upon the protagonist pushing the action forward, whether from her own design or as a reaction to the situation. If the protagonist is not committed to the drama, the audience will not commit to the story. If the plot is merely a natural sequence of incidents, with no real orchestrated rising action, it will be ineffective as well. The incidents may reveal your characters, but if they do not advance the plot a step further towards the crisis, if they do not lead to a big situation, they will be of no dramatic value. Plot is made interesting by the obstacles standing in the protagonist's way. The audience watches with anticipation, in suspense, waiting to see what the hero will do, if he will succeed or fail. If the attainment of the goal is too easy or unrealistic, no one will care. But if the struggle is fierce and suspense intense, the audience will feel satisfied at the end of the film.

The simplest form of plot is one in which the screenwriter places the protagonist in a predicament, keeps him there as long as suspense is maintained, and then extricates him in a surprising but logical way. However, in addition to the bare predicament, the screenwriter must provide interesting and logical reasons why the character falls into the predicament, logical causes for his inability to get out, and finally, a logical but unforeseen escape.

Sometimes your material gives you a ready-made plot. More often, you need to create one where none exists. Once you know your protagonist and his goal, a good starting point is to establish exactly what forces are in conflict with him. Ask yourself, who is trying to accomplish or decide something? What does he wish to do? Who or what opposes the main character? Consider both internal and external forces. What will the result of the commitment, action, struggle be?

Next, determine the moment when conflict begins. This is the initial action or, as defined in the last chapter, the

inciting incident. Then find the moment the character succeeds or fails in his effort: the climax. Both should grow from the character's basic nature and situation.

Now focus on the active moments in your material, the moments of conflict, change, growth, and discovery. These moments are usually the most dramatically significant. A clear understanding of them will help organize the material around the points which will be the most effective to emphasize. These are the moments which should be prolonged within the drama. It can be helpful to list possible scenes, but an actual scene-by-scene outline can be done later.

Think of your film in terms of broad blocks of movement. For example:

–A balanced situation
　　–Some force unbalances the situation

–The character's reaction (or his decision to act)
　　–Consequences of the character's action's

–Re-establishment of balance
　　or

–New Balance
　　or

–Degeneration into chaos

Determine which scenes fall into which categories. Scenes involving the initial conflict belong near the beginning. Scenes dramatizing the protagonist's struggle are usually located in the middle. Scenes showing growth or change in the character will most likely be found in the second half of the story. The most dramatic crisis point undoubtedly relates to the climax which will then result in either the re-establishment of balance or the creation of a new balance or chaos.

This is only a general plan from which to work. Do not be afraid to change, reorganize or even delete scenes as you move ahead. Once a general plan is laid out, creating a more specific scene-by-scene outline of the plot will provide the connections between these broad story beats.

Change and **growth** in the characters need to be shown. **Complications**, **obstacles**, **surprises** that are envisioned have to be incorporated into the line of action. Remember: always keep the conflict front and center in your mind.

As you approach this outline, think in these terms to perfect your plot:

1. **Cause and Effect relationships between scenes**
2. **Rising Conflict** (Attack and Counterattack)
3. **Foreshadowing**

Cause and Effect

All great plots are based on **causality**. Without strong cause-and-effect relationships between scenes, films feel contrived or, worse, boring. Narrative momentum depends upon this relationship between scenes. If cause and effect is poorly developed or does not exist, the audience will lose interest in the film.

Each scene should advance the **action** and cause a **reaction** in the following scene. Since the protagonist's overall story goal is not resolved until the end of the film, we are dramatizing the pursuit of that goal and what happens along the way as a result of it. The successful plot does not focus solely on the scenes showing the active pursuit of the goal or the points of active conflict between the antagonists; it also includes the **reaction** of the main characters, especially the protagonist, to the obstacles, losses, complications, and even successes, he encounters. By showing a character's reaction to the conflict, the audience is better able to identify with him through their own emotional responses to the event. Irwin Blacker said in *The Elements of Screenwriting*, "Plot is more than a pattern of events; it is the ordering of emotions." Without dramatizing the emotional side of the story, any film loses a dimension. If plot is all action and little emotion, it winds up being only melodrama and the audience will be less likely to embrace it fully. A plot pushed by action and not by characters' emotions uses characters as puppets to be manipulated. Director Sidney Lumet said in *Making Movies*, "Drama is when characters move the plot; melodrama, when plot moves characters." Cause-and-effect plotting will naturally lead you to characters moving the plot, because emotions build and force action more realistically than one arbitrary action giving rise to another.

In "Life Lessons," the relationship between the scenes is masterfully handled. Sequences built on action and reaction keep the film focused and moving ahead. One example: After Paulette reconsiders her plan to leave New York and extracts a promise from Lionel that she won't have to sleep with him, the conflict is escalated again in a different manner. A new sequence begins by showing Lionel critiquing Paulette's paintings. Full of self-doubt, Paulette wants more than anything for someone, Lionel, to tell her if she is any good. The one thing Lionel cannot lie about is Art. He says, Art is about having to do it; it's not a choice. And she is, after all, still young. All his pussy-footing around further frustrates Paulette. As Lionel leaves the scene, he kicks himself for what he said, showing his reaction to the increased anxiety he knows he caused for Paulette.

The scene that follows shows Paulette's reaction: In tears, she phones her mother and asks if she can come home. We see her pain, her frustration, while in the background Lionel's music blasts Bob Dylan's "Like a Rolling Stone." The scene helps us empathize with Paulette since most of us have felt pain, frustration and self-doubt. Next, Paulette marches into the studio, angry about the music, about everything, yelling to get his attention. Lionel's unbreakable concentration on his canvas forces her to see the painting taking form underneath his masterful brush strokes. In her face we watch her anger melt away, replaced by awe. She is not in awe of Lionel the person, but Lionel the artist.

In the film's next scene, the two get ready for a party, acting like an old married couple. This scene, which is the beginning of a new sequence, is also the end of the previous one. We learn here that Paulette's response to Lionel's art is to reverse herself and continue working for him. Writer Richard Price wastes no time with a separate scene for Paulette's story point. He lets the audience put two and two together and keeps the plot moving ahead as he now gets ready for the next segment of the story.

All good stories concern themselves with the characters' emotional responses to the action. Good writers know they must show this side of the story to keep the audience relating to the material. It helps us to understand the characters' motivations and to feel empathy for them. As you construct your **plot**, remember to incorporate scenes showing the important characters' responses to the main story points. The questions to ask yourself as you plot with a **cause-and-effect** approach are: What would my character feel as a result of what has just happened? What would he do?

Rising Conflict

Rising conflict is also based on **causality**. We distinguish this type of cause-and-effect relationship from mere action and reaction by the nature of the conflict. Rising conflict entails attack and counterattack. We see this when characters battle each other, most often during the second half of the story. The attacks and counterattacks must become increasingly more serious and threatening to the protagonist as the story progresses. As the battles escalate, they lead directly to the last crisis and climax. Real tension results from a strong rising conflict when the antagonists are locked together and are evenly matched.

In *Peel*, the film begins with the sister (Katie) and brother (Tim) already in conflict. The sister's first line of dialogue from the backseat of the car is a subtle jab at her brother.

"If you don't want other people's opinions, don't ask for them," she says. Silence, except for her nephew (Ben) bouncing an orange off the windshield. She continues: "It was a really scrappy bit of land . . . That's my opinion." At first, Tim does not reply, but tension permeates the car.

Tim's son, Ben, begins peeling the orange and dropping the skin out the window. His father responds by telling the boy not to do it. The boy ignores him and keeps dropping pieces of peel. (This is still action and reaction.) Katie asks the boy for a piece of orange and he screams, "NO!" He jams the orange onto his finger, an action that is too much for his father; who slams on the brakes and orders the boy out of the car to pick up every piece of peel he has dropped. The boy refuses. "We're not leaving here until you pick up every piece of peel on the highway," the father says. Father and son stubbornly stand their ground while, in the car, Katie stews because she wanted to be home by five. Tim tries once more, admonishing the boy that he had better do it. Still, the boy refuses, now gesturing defiantly as if to throw the orange at his father. It's a puny attack from a pint-sized aggressor, but an attack just the same. His father angrily counterattacks by throwing the car into gear and driving straight at the boy! He stops as the bumper rubs up against his son's knees! Now the boy hurls the orange at his father. It splatters against the windshield with a smack, and the boy runs off.

Jane Campion wastes no time building the conflict because she starts in the middle of it, employing a clear attack and counterattack formula. The tension created grabs the audience and makes them pay attention.

Another example comes from "Life Lessons," at the beginning of the second half of the film, in the sequence built around the birthday party. Writer Price further establishes Lionel's stature in the art world as Lionel recounts an obviously oft-told story about how he became an artist. As he tells the tale, he sees a young artist take an interest in Paulette. Jealousy overcomes him and he discovers who the young man is. Lionel whisks Paulette into the bathroom. "People are laughing at you," he tells her, clearly on the attack. He lies about the young man's intentions, which only relieves Paulette's anxiety and makes her laugh because she thought he was going to tell her they were laughing at her work. Lionel thinks his point is considerably worse. Stung, Paulette tries to leave, but Lionel won't let her out of the bathroom. He leaves first, and stands against the door, barring her exit. She has to force her way out of the room. In the next scene, Lionel joins a group singing "Happy Birthday" to the host as Paulette grabs the artist and flaunts her exit in Lionel's face. (This is her counterattack.) Lionel returns home and hears their voices from her room; he turns up the stereo and plunges into his painting.

In the film, *The Thoroughbred*, every one of Kell's actions is an attack; that is the nature of his character. Fitshue has but one counterattack to Kell's threats. He agrees to drug the horse, but he does not go through with it, opting to take a chance and play fair rather than rig a race and give in to Kell's blackmail. In this action, Fitshue reveals his true character.

Foreshadowing the Conflict

To **foreshadow** is to show, indicate or suggest something beforehand. In film or prose, it is the promise of conflict to come. Foreshadowing, too, is based on causality, but the effect is not felt until some time later in the film or story. Since there is little time to waste in a short film, and the writer needs to pin down the problem as soon as possible, foreshadowing isn't as readily employed as other forms of conflict. Nevertheless, foreshadowing does appear in short films, most often when setting up opposing characters. At the beginning of "The Man In The Brooks Brothers Shirt," the young writer sits in a full lounge car, reading her book and talking with other travelers in an amusing, cynical manner. Along comes a businessman who quickly clears the car with his ribald attitude. Only the young woman remains, now happy to be alone with her book, *The Coming Struggle*. The businessman, though, sets his sexual sights on her, and none of her sarcasm or put-downs can dissuade him from his pursuit. This foreshadows a rising conflict between the characters. It makes the audience ask, "What's going to happen next?"

Foreshadowing can be humorous. "Anna Of Milan" opens with a point-of-view shot through the windshield of a Rolls Royce as someone drives around the streets of Milan. The driver's voice belongs to a wealthy, married socialite wearily recounting her obligations for the day and week. As she drives along, she runs stops signs and stop-lights, and barely misses pedestrians crossing the street, drawing incredulous looks. When she makes her rendez-vous with her romantic interest, a handsome writer who gets out of tiny two-door Fiat, the audience knows he is in for trouble.

"Mara Of Rome" utilizes the same trick. It begins by contrasting the virginal young seminary student and the lovely, sensual, clearly sexually active Mara.

Besides promising conflict, **foreshadowing** can be considered a character tool. But the distinction ultimately is unimportant. Character pushes plot, but tools which are used to construct, introduce or motivate character will serve your plot as well.

Exercises

Think of your film's story in broad blocks of movement. What is the original situation and what upsets it? How does the protagonist react? What does she decide to do? What are the consequences of the protagonist's action? How does she react? Where does this action lead? Write the sequence down in a "beat" sheet. (A **beat** is a story point made in a scene or a sequence which moves the plot ahead.)

Now set these main beats aside for a day or two. When you come back to them, contemplate the beats in terms of the rising action, focusing on the cause-and-effect relationships between scenes along with the rising conflict. How does a precipitating action cause a reaction which escalates the conflict to a point where it must be resolved? Try and see a clear line of action between the inciting incident and the climax.

Now return to the exercises at the end of Chapter Three. Using these as a guide, begin to map out a broad, overall story plan. The story tools described in Chapter Three should help create this plan. A thirty-minute film will probably have a movement of seven or eight main beats from start to finish. This will translate into roughly 15 to 20 separate scenes, depending on your writing style. If, for a thirty-minute film, your outline is over 25 scenes, you probably have too much material. But don't worry about it now. In the next chapters, as we look in greater detail at the beginning, middle and end of a short film, you can improve and refine your plot.

PART TWO

Intermediate Steps

5

FADE IN: OPENINGS & THE MAIN EXPOSITION

Finding the best **opening** for any movie is often a trying experience, because it must be visual, convey important information, and be interesting if not arresting it is often challenging to decide how much exposition is necessary, and when and how to convey it. In a short film, with no time to waste, trying to create a compelling opening, get through the **main exposition** and not squander valuable seconds can be even more maddening. Every word, every image, every scene must advance the story toward its conclusion to justify inclusion in the screenplay. And because of the abridged time, anything superfluous to the conflict and our understanding of that conflict detracts from the overall effectiveness of the film.

In this chapter, we look at the elements that help make an opening strong, on its own, and also as an introduction for the main exposition.

The Problem

Answering a few important questions will help you find the best opening for your script. These questions have been asked before, but reviewing them again will give you an idea of your point of departure. What does the protagonist want and why? What is the **main conflict**? (Again, the main conflict is the dramatic problem for the protagonist in the story and may be a person, as in the antagonist, or a situation the hero faces.) Both pose a problem for the protagonist to solve. Putting the problem in the form of a question helps define it.

In "Life Lessons," can Lionel convince Paulette to stay? In "Mara Of Rome," will Mara solve her dispute with Umberto's grandmother? In *The Thoroughbred*, will Fitshue help the bookie fix the race? In *Occurrence At Owl Creek*, will the condemned man escape?

In Chapter Three, we defined a film's the **subproblem** as a conflict of secondary importance that impacts the plot. If a film is going to be framed by a subproblem, it must be translated into the form of a question to be exploited effectively.

The Main Exposition

Knowing the main question as well as the subquestion your story poses for the protagonist helps determine what specific exposition is needed to get the screenplay rolling. In Chapter Three, we defined this exposition—the **main exposition**—as whatever is primary and vital for the audience to know about the protagonist and her problem that can't be shown. Why can't it be shown in a short film? Time constraints: dramatizing the main exposition would delay us reaching the main conflict, which is what really starts the story.

To be sure to grab the audience's attention, the film's plot must begin as close to the introduction of the main conflict as possible. In fact, the **main exposition** must be formulated before you choose the opening images. Often, before starting the story, beginning writers feel the need to tell much more about their protagonists than is necessary; whether they are writing a feature or short screenplay. The discipline that comes with writing a short screenplay will help the writer avoid the common temptation of fully establishing the protagonist before presenting the dramatic problem. An opening sequence will feel aimless if the writer tells us more about the protagonist than what the protagonist's goal is. The purpose of the finished piece is to show the audience who the character is. At the beginning, all we need is a hint. The main conflict, as opposed to offering a character biography (however interesting), makes the audience sit up and take notice.

The main exposition also defines the setting and tone of the film. It introduces the main characters and their central relationships, presents or initiates the conflict, and makes clear whatever is not self-explanatory but necessary to understand. If there is humor in the screenplay, the exposition should be funny—aim for a hearty laugh on page one. If the audience is not quickly oriented to these aspects of the film—time, place, the relationships between characters and the conflict—it will not be able to follow the story. Less important expository details can be spread throughout the film.

Main exposition can be handled in various ways. The Greek chorus is the classic method, as it directly communicates the background on the story and the need to follow the plot. Shakespeare occasionally employed a prologue or soliloquy that was presented to the audience. However, filmmakers of short films, faced with time constraints, need more novel approaches to divulging the main exposition than feature filmmakers. Here are several examples.

Narration

Voice-over **narration** (where the necessary information is expressed quickly and directly by a narrator) is more common in short films than in features. Because the film is so short, this form of exposition is more readily accepted in a short film than in a feature. *The Thoroughbred* employs this technique. Over a street scene of Dublin, the narrator commences the story by telling us a little about the setting and the protagonist, "the honorable Colin Fitshue."

In *Ray's Male Heterosexual Dance Hall*, an Academy Award-winning short written and directed by Bryan Gordon, the protagonist is the narrator and he begins the story by introducing his problem. The scene fades in on a couple of Century City skyscrapers as the narrator announces, "I used to feel I was a part of those buildings. After all, I once had an office there. OK, I didn't have an office with a view, but I was headed for a view. A good view." The camera cranes down to show the protagonist, Sam, sitting on a bench. "That, of course, was before Fedtech became Welpeck and left me out of a job." Out of work, Sam needs to find a good job. With the arrival of an old friend, the story is set in motion. Sam's narration continues, providing humorous commentary on what he encounters.

On-screen narrators can also appear. Rod Serling opened *The Twilight Zone* on screen, disclosing fundamental information needed to begin the story. Serling's style of exposition was originally an inventive twist to the introductions given by off-screen announcers on many of the old anthology television series.

On-screen narration is taken to its zenith in the film "The Dutch Master." The story is told by multiple narrators, on screen and off, talking directly to the audience. The film begins with a shot of a man sitting in a dental chair, his mouth wide open. The narration starts as the camera pans over X rays, dental equipment and the sterile office until it finally introduces us to Teresa, an attractive dental hygienist. "We've known Teresa for like, what, six years?" a woman says over the images.

"Longer," answers another unseen woman.

"And I'm telling you, it just wasn't like her."

"Not at all."

As the two women relate their story, the action shows the three friends and fellow dental hygienists doing what they usually do, hurrying across the street to eat lunch on the steps of the Metropolitan Museum of Art. Then the action shifts to the two narrators, sitting on the steps of the museum and eating hot dogs. Teresa is missing. Dorothy and Kim address the audience through the camera as it hovers before them like an old friend.

"We eat here practically every day," says Dorothy. "Unless, of course it was raining, then we'd go back and eat in Dr. Roserman's office but he would always complain about Teresa's chili and onions, saying the smell was bad for business. Then one day, it must of been four weeks ago, for no apparent reason, Teresa says she wants to go inside."

On screen we see Teresa enter the museum alone. She wanders about as the narration continues, the two friends commenting upon her actions. As the story continues, more characters are introduced, each adding his or her particular view of events. The only character who never utters a word is Teresa. By contrasting Teresa's actions with the others' accounts of events, the filmmakers illustrate how little each knows or understands Teresa. Her actions are our only clue to what is going on with her.

Another variation of voice-over narration is used in "Anna Of Milan." The film opens with a POV shot through the windshield of a Rolls Royce. A woman's voice murmurs, as if we're hearing her thoughts, while she drives through the streets of Milan. "Ah," she sighs deeply. "The traffic is a mess here this early in the morning. Hmmm. Easy does it, easy does it. Why don't the working classes stay home and sleep . . . At least on Sunday morning!" From Anna's vocal **exposition** we learn that she is an unhappily married socialite who is fed up with her life. Wearily recounting her many obligations for the day and week—charities, dinner parties, hairdresser, dress fittings—she drives, paying little attention to pedestrians and ignoring stop signs. Finally, she cries: "Enough, enough! Enough!

No more. To hell with it! I'm going to make a clean break. Randall, Randall," she purrs. "Right now I don't even remember the color of his eyes—the darling. The finest person I know—so generous, independent. So totally unspoiled, the dear boy," she giggles. "With those incredibly short socks of his . . . " Up ahead, a tiny Fiat is parked on a side street. "There he is. There he is," she says, and she pulls up in her Rolls behind him.

The contrast between her words and the action creates a humorous tone for the film. She drives along, talking to herself as if she were in sole possession of the road; she runs stops signs and stoplights. People look, then immediately dash out of her way. There is a reaction shot of a policeman taking down her car license as she rolls through yet another red light. This appropriately punctuates the sequence.

The important information to be dispensed is that she's married, wealthy and unhappy. She is completely self-absorbed though she would never admit it, and we've joined her in her Rolls en route to a tryst. The beginning monologue and action give us the exposition of the situation— and they set the tone of the piece. The story that follows grows out of the mismatched personalities of the paramours. We know our story and main character are humorous.

Written Presentation

In the very short film, *Peel*, Jane Campion uses a written presentation of the main exposition. Cards appear on the screen, intercut with opening credits and shots of a highway flashing by. All are punctuated by the sound of the radio or highway noise. The first card appears:

AN EXERCISE IN DISCIPLINE

Road signs swish by, then the title flashes in big bold letters that fill up the screen:

PEEL

After another flashing shot of the highway and a list of the players, a card appears identifying the characters and representing the relationships between them.

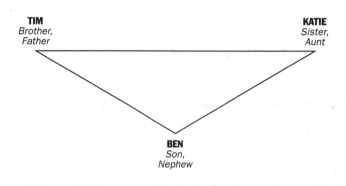

Another highway shot speeds by, and the final card comes up:

A TRUE STORY/A TRUE FAMILY

The film, which is under ten minutes, gives us the necessary information in less than a minute. The cards waste no time, allowing the story to speed ahead into the main conflict. Because the cards flash by so quickly, the effect is almost subliminal.

Visual Dramatization

Occurrence At Owl Creek presents a visual dramatization of the initial information. The film opens with the camera moving over a burnt-out landscape before dawn. It lingers for a moment on a sign hammered to a tree trunk:

ORDER

ANY CIVILIAN

CAUGHT INTERFERING WITH

THE RAILROAD BRIDGES

TUNNELS OR TRAINS WILL BE

SUMMARILY HANGED

THE 4TH OF APRIL, 1862

Though a written presentation, the sign is only part of the main exposition; it also serves to establish the time. A subsequent group of images establishes place. As a low roll on a drum sounds, an owl hoots, a bugle calls, and a Union officer stands on a bridge barking orders. Nearby, a sentinel, with a rifle, watches from above. This sets the film's time; it takes place during the U.S. Civil War.

We know time and place, but the exposition is not complete because we do not yet know our protagonist or his conflict. Union riflemen march across the bridge and come to attention before the officer. A sergeant carries a length of rope to a bearded man in civilian clothes who stands at the edge of the bridge, face beaded with sweat. His fine clothes indicate he is a gentleman. His gentle, expressive face contrasts with those of the harsh Union soldiers. Hands and feet are tied. The sergeant efficiently loops the rope into a hangman's noose and tightens the knot. Soldiers push the prisoner onto a plank suspended over a river. As the sergeant secures the noose around the prisoner's neck, the man gasps and looks wildly about.

The conflict is fully established. What will happen to the man? Will he escape? Will someone come to his rescue? The entire opening, in less than five minutes, gives all that is necessary to begin the thirty-minute film. No names, no dialogue, only a series of powerful images, heightened by the sound track, that leads to the terrifying problem the condemned man faces.

Exposition in Dialogue

In many films, scenes with dialogue convey parts of the main exposition. In "Life Lessons," after the opening establishes artist and studio, the story starts with the sound of the elevator bell. In contrast to the disheveled artist we have seen, a neatly groomed man rides up in the cage. He is an art dealer, Philips, here to see Lionel's new work. "There's nothing to see, it's the emperor's new clothes, I'm gonna get slaughtered," Lionel croaks, refusing to let Phillips out of the elevator. Philips tries to get Lionel to come to lunch, presumably to loosen him up, but Lionel says he must pick up his assistant at the airport. "I don't know why she can't take a cab like everyone else," the artist confesses. After a pause, Philips proceeds delicately, inquiring when he will be able to return and see the work. He says softly: "The show's in three weeks, you know." Panic flares in Lionel's eyes and he hits the switch that sends the man down the chute. "Ah, Lionel," says Philips in exasperation. "Lionel! You go through this before every show! I'm talking twenty years of this! Now get to know yourself a little better, Lionel!"

By the end of this scene, we know about the impending art show and Lionel's assistant. So far, we have half of the important information necessary to begin the story, all given in one scene. What makes the scene work well is the conflict, already established between the two men. Their common history, including the coming exhibition, is their **backstory**. The art dealer desiring entrance into the studio and the panic-stricken artist keeping him prisoner in the elevator dramatize their opposition.

The next scene reveals the second key piece of the main exposition: Lionel's assistant, with whom he has been having an affair, is leaving New York because the romance is over. Lionel doesn't want her to go. His dramatic problem is how to keep her in Manhattan and prepare for his upcoming show.

The Main Exposition's Relationship to the Climax & Theme

The main exposition has a direct relationship to the film's climax as well as an indirect relationship to the film's theme. The problem posed at the beginning of the story is the one that needs to be solved or answered at the end. If Richard Price wants Lionel's loss of Paulette at the end to mean something, Lionel's total infatuation for her must be set up at the beginning, even if the author ironically undercuts the pain of Lionel's loss in the resolution.

If Mara in "Mara Of Rome" is going to solve her problem with the old woman, the dispute has to be set up at the start. Even though the focus of Mara's dramatic problem changes from grandmother to grandson, the basic problem doesn't: If the grandson doesn't return to the seminary, Mara surely will be blamed. The subproblem of "Mara Of Rome"— the story that asks if Rosconi ever gets Mara in bed—never changes and it is answered in the resolution.

If a film is about self-indulgence or delusion, or honesty and faith, or about the inability of families to communicate, this too needs to be revealed or foreshadowed at the start. Just as the audience should become acquainted with the protagonist's problem early on, the same is true of the theme. The viewers will grasp the film's intent only if the theme is introduced early.

Viewers do not need to be directly told what the film is about, but they need hints, they need clues. If ten people see a film and have ten different interpretations of what it was about, the film's theme could not have been very well-developed.

Exposition, particularly in dialogue, continues without interruption until the climax of the movie, for writers are always exposing characters and plot. This type of exposition also can illuminate the backstory, the action that happened before the film started. Besides the **main exposition**, other information can be given as it is needed, or introduced when the viewer needs it to understand what will happen next. In a short film, gratuitous information is worse than superfluous; it delays necessary action and obscures the information that is truly important.

When working on the **main exposition**, think in these terms:

1. What is essential to be revealed?
2. What can be held back?
3. What can be implied?

Holding back or implying certain information can help to maintain tension for the audience and will get the viewers to anticipate what will happen next. If you reveal too much, the audience will become bored. If, in "Life Lessons," Lionel said to Paulette at the airport: "I need the friction of our crazy relationship to help me paint," the story would have been short-circuited and their subsequent fights would have lacked tension.

Opening the Movie

Good openings elicit our curiosity, raising more questions than they answer. They unlock doorways allowing us to enter into a slightly different world than our own. Good openings are visual, utilizing the language of the medium— images and sounds—to conjure feelings and carry the story's mood to the audience.

Point of Decision

Screen stories must open near a point of decision or crisis; the more dramatic the decision or crisis, the better the opening. This crisis or decision is, of course, connected to the main conflict. The film can open just before this moment, exactly at the moment or just after it. Out of this life-changing situation, the hero's goal emerges.

Life-changing events include:
> starting school
> getting a driver's license
> graduating high school
> starting college
> birth
> marriage

> losing or quitting a job
> divorce
> funeral

In other words, something is about to happen, to change.

The life-changing situation in "Life Lessons" established in the first scene is the art exhibition for which Lionel has nothing worth showing. He is understandably panicked because this could mean failure in his career. In the second scene, when he picks up his assistant Paulette at the airport, he learns his love affair with her is over. Lionel's day goes from bad to worse.

In *Occurrence At Owl Creek*, the protagonist is about to be hanged. It's hard to find anything more life-changing or dramatic than that.

Change in the Environment

A Change In The Environment can affect the protagonist directly or indirectly; it also can introduce a new element which directly effects the protagonist. A change can be represented by a war, a natural disaster, a death in a family.

The Red Balloon begins with an image of a cold and wet cobblestone courtyard dominated by large old houses. The atmosphere is gray and lonely. A young boy, Pascal, steps into frame, carrying a briefcase. He is dwarfed by the buildings. He lingers at the top of a staircase to pet a cat, then goes on his way until, halfway down, something catches his eye. He climbs a lamppost and retrieves a red balloon. The balloon starkly contrasts the world around him. It is large, round, bright red, the color of life. The story that follows shows Pascal struggling to keep this new element—the red balloon—in his life.

In "Mara Of Rome," Umberto's arrival at his grandmother's house indirectly creates the situation for Mara. Had he not arrived, the grandmother's disdain for Mara and her profession would not have hit the breaking point.

The Protagonist

Many films open by introducing the protagonist which is as good a place as any to begin. As in real life, first meetings make strong impressions, so the screenwriter must show the audience right away what is important, unique and/or interesting about the protagonist, especially in relationship to the story. This is really the beginning of his or her character arc, however small it may be in a short film. A good question to ask is: What is essential for the audience to know about this character at the start? Even if the sole purpose of the film is to peel away layers to illustrate who the character is at heart, the protagonist's outer facade must be illustrated first, so the later contrast with his inner "essence" can be demonstrated.

"Life Lessons" opens with the camera zeroing in on different objects in the studio—paints, empty canvases, stereo boombox, Napoleon cognac—until it arrives on Lionel, alone in the big studio, disheveled and desperate. The sound of the elevator bell introduces the conflict (with his art dealer) that is foreshadowed by the desperate look in Lionel's eyes.

The writer must also consider how he wants to present the main character to the audience. Does he want the audience to laugh at the protagonist or pity him? Should we take him seriously or write him off? Does the writer want the audience to identify with the protagonist or objectify him? These questions relate to the tone of the film. If the tone is satiric or broadly humorous, the audience will not be as closely involved with the characters. A serious or ironic tone allows the audience more emotional involvement in the film. How the audience views the character depends on how the writer presents him. As a writer, you need to be clear about your feelings for the protagonist in order to communicate them effectively to the audience.

Scene Considerations

In terms of scene construction, there are specific considerations for the opening that can be highlighted here although Part Three covers the actual writing of scenes (craft and technique) in more depth.

Several elements go into making an interesting and effective opening. First, does the scene raise a question in the minds of the viewers about what will happen in the story? If the opening scene does not raise a question, where and when will the question be raised? Introducing the dramatic question early will help gain the audience's attention, because they will want to know how this problem will be resolved. The question raised in the first scene in "Life Lessons" is about Lionel's up-coming art exhibition: Will he have any work to show? The question raised in the next scene is about his relationship with Paulette: Will she leave?

Next, you want to know if there is action in the scene to make it interesting. Is there conflict? The opening scene in "Life Lessons," though all exposition, is relayed through conflict between Lionel and Philip. Philip wants out of the elevator, but Lionel keeps him in. This is the action that represents the conflict between them. The two men aren't yelling at each other, but each has a different scene goal. Like a story goal, a scene goal is what a character wants to accomplish during the action within the scene. (More on this in Part Three, on constructing a scene.)

Action in a scene can be physical. What interesting thing can the character be doing on the screen? In *Peel*, after the opening credits and exposition, the scene starts with a boy's feet propped on the dashboard of a moving car. This may or may not be adolescent impudence, but when the boy starts bouncing an orange between his feet with a THUNK, THUNK, THUNK, and throwing it against the windshield and rolling it down his legs, we know the driver of the car will start to grit his teeth.

So, even before taking a look around the car, the action has our attention. Once we've taken that look, the sound becomes more striking because it accentuates the tension between Tim, the boy's father who drives, and Katie, Tim's sister, who sits sullenly in the backseat.

"If you don't want other people's opinions, don't ask for 'em," she says. Silence, except for the thunk, thunk, thunk of the boy's orange. Then: "It was a really scrappy bit of land . . . That's my opinion." The brother does not reply but the tension level rises in the car.

The idea is to show the problem, not tell it. The more originally you can show it, the better. Viewers will believe the conflict more readily if they witness the problem themselves.

Foreshadowing is a more subtle method to showing conflict and can be seen in "Mara Of Rome." After panning across a plaza, the camera comes to rest on the balcony of a high-rise apartment where a young priest paces, looking at his bible. Near him, an old lady feeds birds and an old man paints. Across the patio, on another high-rise balcony, a woman wrapped only in a white towel comes out of her apartment carrying two new plants for her garden planters. She tosses one of the wrappers over the side before seeing the young priest watching her. Because her view is obscured, she doesn't realize at first that he is a priest, thinking only that he is a young man. She takes a gardening tool to turn the soil of the new plants as she checks him out. He is clearly taken with her beauty. From her new vantage point, she sees his collar and realizes he is a priest. She smiles at him, amused by what she gleans in his face.

The contrast between the young priest and the beautiful, sensual woman creates a subtle tension in the viewer's mind and foreshadows more conflict to come when these two characters come together. The actual conflict, we cannot predict, but in the next scene, we learn Mara is a prostitute with a high-class clientele. This serves to up the ante, even though we aren't sure of which direction the story will take.

Another consideration for a strong opening is to ask if there's anything about the character we can learn now that can be utilized at the end. The earlier the writer shows us an important detail about the protagonist that affects the outcome of the story, the less contrived it feels. The first scene of "Life Lessons" does two things: First, it sets up the art exhibition at the film's end. Second, a piece of exposition shouted by Philip as he rides the elevator down at the end of the scene gives us a clue about what might happen. Philip shouts, "Ah, Lionel, Lionel! You go through this before every show! I'm talking twenty years of this! Now, get to know yourself a little better, Lionel! You can pull it off. You always do!"

It's not until the very end that we understand the full ramification of his statement. Lionel does "pull it off." His exhibition is a complete success. But it is not until he meets the beautiful young artist in the last scene that we comprehend what the story means. As we watch his infatuation with this young woman and hear him offer her a job with the same lines he gave Paulette, we understand this is Lionel's style, his technique, his *modus operandi*. He goes "through this before every show," Philip had said. All of Lionel's declarations of love for Paulette weren't necessarily meaningless; but perhaps what he said to her in the climax was true, that his art and relationships feed off each other. He needs one to fuel the other. After all, he's been married and divorced four times since before Paulette was born. Therefore, the little piece of exposition given at the beginning, when taken in the context of the whole, helps give final shape to the overall meaning of the film.

As a story develops, an opening image or idea that began the whole process may have to be scrapped in favor of something that gets the plot moving faster. Though some screenwriters begin writing before they have thoroughly worked out their plot and story, they generally must revise extensively once a first draft is completed. A writer may discover many interesting details this way, but a lot of time can be wasted, too. You'll always need to rewrite to improve your screenplay, but you can keep rewriting to a minimum by having as good an understanding of your story as possible before writing your first draft.

Exercises

Consider the opening of your film. Ask:

1. What is the problem driving it?
    a. Frame it in the form of a question that conveys a sense of the main action the protagonist must take. (Will Lionel convince Paulette to stay? Will the condemned man escape?)
    b. If there is a subproblem, pose it in the form of a question. (Will Rosconi bed Mara?)
2. Express what you think are the most important parts of the main exposition.
    a. Can this information be conveyed without dialogue?
    b. If so, which parts?
    c. How can you most creatively handle this exposition?
3. If you only have one or two scenes to start your movie, what's the most dramatic (or comedic, i.e., showstopping way) to open it?
    a. Is there action in the scenes?
    b. Where is the conflict coming from?
    c. Is something going on that causes tension or gets us wondering what is going on?
    d. If your story is subtle, can you foreshadow the conflict by contrasting opposites? Is there any other way?
4. Is there something thematic which can be dropped into the opening to hint at the direction of the film?

Now, start your plot outline. Visualize the separate scenes as if you were seeing the movie. Each time you change locales, you must start a new scene. For a film that is thirty minutes or less, allow no more than three scenes to kick off your film. And if it is less than fifteen minutes, you must introduce the conflict in the second scene, at the very latest.

The opening should poise the plot on a specific line of

action which will take it to the mid-point of the script. If you have trouble finding the best opening two or three scenes, use as many as it takes right now, with the idea that once the story gets rolling, you will come back and pare it down.

6

THE MIDDLE— KEEPING THE STORY ALIVE

As in a feature, the **middle** section of a short film often presents the greatest difficulties. Once the story is set in motion, it can be frustrating to juggle the important plot elements—action, character and theme—so that the story keeps moving and has meaning. The middle is generally the longest section of a film and the hardest to keep focused. But the middle is where the battle is won or lost. If the middle wanders, doesn't move or skips over important developments, the film will lose its audience. Filmgoers need to move with the characters and conflict, yet still be surprised and entertained. If the middle is not focused on the story or developments seem haphazard, the audience will lose patience and interest in the film.

Chapters Three and Four laid a foundation for story structure and discussed its tools for construction. In this chapter, we take a closer look at a few of those tools, and some new ones, to see how they enhance and strengthen the middle section of a film.

Suspense

In Chapter Three, we labeled the **middle** section the "**rising action**." This was described as the course of action the protagonist takes to achieve his goal and the **obstacles** he faces as a result. A few of the screenwriter's tools discussed in that chapter were antagonists, obstacles, complications, reversals and crises; a story cannot be constructed without some combination of these elements. The most important elements they contribute are **conflict**, **suspense** and **surprise**. A detailed discussion of conflict was given in Chapter Four. Now let's turn to suspense and surprise.

According to the *Concise Dictionary of Literary Terms*, **suspense** is a mental state of "uncertainty, excitement, or indecision." Film suspense should leave the audience waiting for an outcome of events. As the audience waits, they should wonder and anticipate what will happen to the protagonist and the other characters in the story. "Suspense," says the *Concise Dictionary*, "is a quality of tension in a plot which sustains interest and makes the readers and viewers ask 'what happens next?' "

Tension and **suspense** are created in many ways. Hitchcockian suspense (named for the master of the macabre, Alfred Hitchcock) lets the audience in on issues or incidents the characters don't know about, then exploits the audience's anticipation of how the characters will react when they find out. At the beginning, the audience is always on the side of the hero. And as he struggles to overcome the problem, he should gain the audience's interest and respect. But as the story moves forward, tension and suspense need to be stoked like a fire in order to maintain them. Here are some ways.

The Antagonist

A strong **antagonist** contributes to a film's tension and suspense. Since the antagonist best represents the hero's problem, the stronger he is, the greater the suspense will be as to whether or not the hero will succeed. A good rule of thumb is to introduce the antagonist at the earliest logical moment. No one should sit around waiting for suspense to begin. We can only wonder what will happen once the conflict has been introduced.

The Dreadful Alternative

To compound suspense, put the hero in **jeopardy** and keep him there. Jeopardy for the protagonist can be personal, as in the risk of losing love or respect. It can be physical. An obvious negative consequence awaiting the hero if he should fail to solve the story's problem will add more suspense. Setting up such a dreadful fate helps create automatic suspense from that moment on; the price of failure for the hero must be high in order to generate genuine suspense. Therefore, some presentation of this negative consequence early on will lace your story with suspense for its entire length.

In "Life Lessons," if Lionel can't convince Paulette to stay, the cost for him is loneliness, or so it appears. Later in the story, when she stays, we see that her platonic presence will mean sexual frustration for Lionel. But there's also the problem of the exhibition. If Lionel should stop painting for the exhibition, his career will suffer. In *The Thoroughbred*, Fitshue risks his reputation and livelihood if he refuses to go along with Kell's plan. In *Occurrence At Owl Creek*, a man's life is at stake.

Unexpected Complications

The unexpected **complication** adds suspense to any story, because a sudden surprise produces a new, additional obstacle for the hero, thus keeping the tension mounting. In "Life Lessons," young men clearly threaten Lionel's appetite for young women. So, the performance artist Gregory Stark complicates matters for Lionel, as does the young "graffiti" artist Ruben Torro. How Lionel deals with Paulette and her suitor reveals a lot about his character. The appearance of a young man, even Paulette's brother, always leads to real angst for Lionel.

In *Occurrence At Owl Creek*, the protagonist faces a snake in the surging river while Union soldiers shoot at him from the bridge. He dives deep to avoid this complication and is swept up in the current, further complicating his escape.

In *The Thoroughbred*, Fitshue is able to make it look like he's favoring another horse in the big race, as Kell wants him to, by placing Miss Kenneally's bet for her. But this causes Kell to distrust Fitshue. He demands Fitshue drug Minstrel as insurance the horse won't win, setting another complication for Fitshue.

Suspense Killers

The worst enemy of suspense is **predictability**. If the audience easily foresees what's going to happen and their expectations are met without surprise, they become bored. While it's true that the possibility of imminent crises needs to be foreshadowed, it is the possibility, not the certainty of these crises, which gives rise to suspense and **anticipation**. We know conflict is going to take place, but if we can predict how and when it will happen, and who gets hurt, the story loses interest, momentum and value.

A protagonist who is so strong and smart that he can solve any problem through might or intellect will not engender much suspense. Therefore, the protagonist needs to be challenged. The greater the odds against the hero succeeding, the more the audience will root for him to prevail.

Another impediment to suspense is the early loss of the antagonist. To keep suspense alive, the antagonist needs to be viable until the climax of the film. If she is removed from contention in the story before the final crisis and climax, momentum will be slowed and suspense will be lost.

Surprise

Surprise is a key element of successful screenwriting and filmmaking, as it plays a part in maintaining suspense. It helps stimulate our curiosity regarding the story, making us ask over and over again that critical question: "What is going to happen next?" If we are not surprised, the film will not hold us.

Surprise means "to take unawares or to affect with unexpected wonder." When a plot takes a sudden turn in an unexpected direction, it can surprise us. When a character behaves in a startling way or does something seemingly inexplicable, it can astonish us. As a film progresses, the audience needs to be frequently surprised by the characters and action. As the end nears, surprises must intensify. The final surprise is often the revelation or epiphany, which is really the whole point of the story. We'll talk about this in more depth in the next chapter.

In "Life Lessons," what is the first surprise after the initial scene establishing Lionel as a desperate man? It is the following scene, at the airport, where he has gone to pick up Paulette. In the previous scene he tells Philip that he can't go to lunch because he has to pick up his assistant. "I don't know why she can't take a cab like everyone else," he shrugs. But when we see Lionel at the airport, waiting anxiously, filmed in slow motion, emphasizing both his impatience and his total concentration on her, we realize something is not what it seems. When she gets off the plane, what he lives for has arrived. Paulette's reaction when she sees him contrasts his completely. "Oh, shit," she says.

"Life Lessons" is constantly surprising us with Lionel's behavior, and Paulette's, too. In nearly every scene, Lionel does something startling, acting in a seemingly contradictory way, and this is one of the major reasons why the film keeps our interest.

In *Peel*, both the father and the son surprise us with their behavior. Our first surprise is when the father pushes

107

his son out the door and tells him to pick up every piece of orange peel he has dropped on the highway. This is a rather astonishing request, but given the circumstances, we accept it. However, the boy runs in the opposite direction, to the front of the car. As his father admonishes him to obey, the boy cocks his arm defiantly, threatening to throw the orange at his father (behind the windshield). The boy's action surprises not only his father, but us, too. When the father responds with his own threat, by inching the car up against the boy's knees, we are startled, if not amazed. The boy runs off and the plot now takes a new direction.

In *The Red Balloon*, when Pascal's mother puts the balloon out the window of their apartment, the act is unforeseen and shocking because it is so mean-spirited. But when the balloon waits at the window for the boy, we are even more surprised. The boy sneaks the balloon back inside, and we, the audience, share his unexpected happiness.

In *Occurrence At Owl Creek*, the plot takes a sudden and unexpected turn when the rope breaks and the condemned man falls into the river. We are further amazed by the length of time the man lasts underwater. He struggles with the ropes and finally gets them off, emerging into a startling clear perspective of life around him. After the filmmaker drives home his point, we are suddenly made aware of the Union soldiers still on the bridge. Men holler, in an audio equivalent to slow motion, gunshots ring out, and now the man is racing for his life. All of this runs counter to our rational expectations and so surprises us and holds our interest.

Chapter Four discussed **probability** in relationship to plot. Probability is not **predictability**. Whatever surprises the characters come up with, whichever direction the plot turns, these elements must be rooted in the realm of the probable: the surprises must have a reality to them within the context of the story. Surprise keeps us off balance, it keeps us guessing, and it helps hold our attention because we cannot predict what is going to happen next.

The Reversal

One of the strongest surprises occurring in a film takes place when everything seems to be headed in one direction; then something happens and suddenly the film is headed in the opposite direction. This is called a **reversal**: good fortune may change into bad or bad into good. More often than not, the situation created is not only unanticipated but unwanted.

In feature films, a major reversal may force the protagonist to go in an entirely new, and unforeseen, direction, while a minor reversal might cause the hero to reconsider his plan of action and discard it in favor of something else. Most feature films have at least one major reversal, usually near the end of the middle section (often referred to as the second act). A major reversal in a feature can have dramatic implications for the protagonist and cause radical changes. Minor reversals in features occur without the same consequences for the protagonist and the plot. Short films employ major reversals, too, but they come at a different point in the action.

The Reversal in Relationship to the Midpoint

In a short film, a reversal is most often found at the **midpoint** of the plot, when one of the main characters, the protagonist or antagonist, shifts course, thereby resulting in a change of direction for the film. In Chapter Three, we already discussed the reversal at the midpoint of "Life Lessons." The reversal comes when Paulette is ostensibly headed home, then changes her mind after becoming deeply affected while watching Lionel paint.

In "Mara Of Rome," the midpoint reversal occurs when the relationship between Mara and the old grandmother changes from two enemies to two friends. The old woman's anguish melts Mara's anger and she goes from wanting to hurt the old woman to vowing to help her.

In "The Blue Dog," from *Especially On Sunday*, Amleto reaches his limit with the dog at the midpoint. About to shoot the howling mongrel outside his apartment, he finds

109

he can't do it and he puts the rifle down. But a neighbor shoots the dog instead. Amleto is surprised, and then sad. In the morning when he goes to find the carcass, he discovers a trail of blood: the animal is alive! Suddenly joyous, he takes off to find the animal. This becomes the second half of the story, as Amleto now tries to find the animal he worked so hard to destroy in the first half of the film.

The Reversal in Relationship to the Setup & Climax

Sometimes we see a **reversal** within the **setup**. In *Occurrence At Owl Creek*, the broken rope is the catalyst of the story. Until this moment, it appears the man is going to hang. When the rope breaks, startling us, the film becomes one about whether or not he will escape. The reversal is used again at the climax of the film, when we realize that all we have seen has occurred within the man's mind during the last seconds of his life. It is a powerful climax, again startling us, and it drives home the film's theme.

Emotion & Reversals

Reversals work best when emotion connects with the action and/or consequences of the action. Emotion can fuel and cause a reversal; emotion can result from a change in the situation. Emotion adds depth to the reversal and enhances the drama.

In "Life Lessons," Paulette not only reverses her decision to leave, but emotionally she leaves her despair and renews her conviction to her art. In "The Blue Dog," Amleto's anger turns to sorrow when the neighbor shoots the dog. In the morning when he discovers the animal lives, his sorrow changes to happiness. In "Mara Of Rome," the old grandmother's despair causes Mara's anger to turn to sympathy. All these moments are emotional reversals, as well as plot reversals. They change the direction of the plot in unforeseen ways and propel the characters into the second half of the story.

The Pseudo Solution

Another plot strategy for the middle section might be termed the "pseudo solution" of the story problem. Here, the initial story question or problem is answered or solved, but, in most cases, the repercussions are more unanticipated problems. The pseudo solution usually takes place at the plot's midpoint, so the second half of the plot must show the effect of solving the problem for the protagonist.

In "The Man In The Brooks Brothers Shirt," the plot question seems to be, will our heroine resist Jerry? When she agrees to go to his compartment for a drink, the audience knows the odds are shifting. It makes no difference that he's promised no hanky-panky; saying no but meaning yes is a tactic employed by both sexes. The more she drinks, it seems the less likely she will be able to resist a lecherous advance. The film appears set on its course—will he or won't he bed her? Instead of waiting until the end to resolve this, a pseudo solution occurs halfway through the film when she wakes up with a hangover in his berth and is unable to believe she has slept with him.

The real surprise comes in the second half of the film, which deals with the consequences of her actions. Jerry now tells our unnamed and hungover heroine that he's in love with her; he will leave his wife and children to take care of her in New York while he seeks a divorce! All this from a man who is the antithesis of everything she believes in—a class enemy! But he offers her security, family, home—things that, as she gets older, are starting to have greater meaning. The plot question now evolves into a new, unexpected conundrum. What will the worldly-wise, unsentimental leftist do? The second half of the film answers this question, and in the answer, the protagonist's character and, ultimately, what the film is about, are both defined.

When what we believe to be the main plot concern is resolved at the midpoint, in a pseudo solution, the story that emerges is usually more complex than one whose dramatic problem has remained unaltered. Why? Because the unsubtle problem posed in the setup is now dispensed with and the ramifications are more complex problems (outlined in the entire first half of the story). In "The Man In The Brooks Brothers Shirt," our heroine first answers a simple question of whether she will give in to Jerry; then she addresses the more subtle aspects of her feminine character. Whether she'll put out becomes a rumination on the possibility of emotional security with an intellectual foe.

Sometimes, as in *Twist Of Fate*, the protagonist solves his problem at the midpoint. The audience follows the film to see what the protagonist will do next. The protagonist, William, is homeless and schizophrenic. Outside the posh Beverly Hills Hotel, William asks a woman with her daughter if she can "spare a little change for something to eat?" The woman ignores him, but the little girl can't. As a Rolls Royce pulls up, the little girl slips off her pearl bracelet and drops it on the ground. He picks it up and tries to give it back. But the woman, ignorant of her daughter's compassion, refuses to look at him, and they drive away.

William now has something of value, but the question is, what will he do with it? Conflict dogs him in many ways. First, police appear. He's then intimidated by a group of bikers. Next, he almost gives the bracelet to a blind man. Finally, he winds up at a pawn shop, where he exchanges the bracelet for $200 and a white suit. This occurs at the midpoint. Now, he has more than a little money for food, and a white suit. The question is, what will he do with it all?

Solving the initial story problem halfway through the film can have liberating results. A plot confined by a single problem will be vivified by resolving the problem well before the climax; this triggers new, unforeseen problems and offers new possibilities for the second half. A pseudo solution makes a film more lifelike: Often, the greatest problems are posed only after we have gotten what we thought we wanted.

Exercises

In the exercise at the end of Chapter Five, you focused on the beginning of the plot of your screenplay. Now, it is time to juggle the middle section, or the rising action, to keep it escalating. Though the exact number of scenes will vary with each film, the middle section of a thirty-minute film (i.e., approximately a thirty-page screenplay) will be ten to thirteen scenes. In a fifteen-minute film, the middle will probably be five to seven scenes (and, if there is one main locale, as in *The Lunch Date*, five to seven main beats will exist within that extended scene).

Let's start with a few questions you can apply to the work on your plot that is already completed.

1. Have you introduced the conflict clearly and strongly enough to cause the protagonist to act?
   a. If so, what does he do?
   b. Will he face a consequence should he fail to achieve his goal?

2. In taking action, what obstacle does the protagonist encounter?
   a. Is there more than one kind?
   b. Does the protagonist face inner as well as outer obstacles?
   c. What is the best way to show his inner conflict?

3. Are there complications for the protagonist (or antagonist)?
   a. Do these consequences pay off later in the story?

4. Can you envision a strong midpoint in the plot, where the action suddenly reverses direction and surprises the audience?
   a. What would happen if the plot question posed at the beginning is answered at the midpoint and the rest of the screenplay deals with the consequences?
   b. What direction would the plot take as a result?
   c. Whatever happens at the midpoint, how does this lead to the most dramatic (i.e., life-chang-

113

ing) moment for the character within the plot?
d. Is this a crisis or the climax of the screenplay?

Using the answers to these questions, begin to organize the material. You want to create a line of action heading first to the midpoint of the story, then the climax. Look for a specific midpoint, especially a reversal. The line of action which starts at the inciting incident (the moment when the plot problem is exposed) should drive toward the midpoint, ideally creating one expectation in the mind of the audience while delivering another.

The focus of the next segment of action is the final crisis leading to a climax. The protagonist still needs complications and obstacles to face in the second half. Remember to create cause-and-effect relationships between the scenes and to orchestrate a rising conflict through an attack and counterattack strategy between the protagonist and antagonist.

Write your scene outline down, continuing the numbering from your first two or three scenes at the opening. You may first need to write down everything that occurs to you as the protagonist moves from inciting incident toward climax. Then, go back and cull through the scenes, using the most effective and dramatic moments. You probably won't need all the material you create in your first pass. Many transitions won't be necessary. You may discover scene repetitions. Make connections between scenes stronger by cutting material irrelevant to the main action, after you can see what that storyline is.

Don't rush the process, and don't be afraid to rework the plot line you created. This is going to be the backbone of your work.

7

FADE OUT: REVELATION, CLIMAX & RESOLUTION

In the final stretch of the screenplay, writers often feel energized. The words all screenwriters long to type dangle in front of them. "FADE OUT, THE END" signals the completion of the task. In the rush to get to these words, all writers, especially beginning writers, can become careless with the final section of the screenplay. Here, traditionally, the hero deflects the villain with "a mighty blow." But often in short screenplays, instead of being the most forceful and consequential moment of the screenplay, the climactic chase often runs out of gas. Short films are prone to anti-climaxes because the nature of them (from more limited budgets to less time for building the drama) requires a more subtle **resolution** than does long-form drama. A final twist or irony or character **revelation** proves ideal as opposed to a triumph on the battlefield.

The ending is, of course, why we come to the party in

the first place. It is the reason, the purpose, the ambition of the film. In the ending, the writer reveals what the experience has been about. In great films, whether short or long, the ending gives the audience more than entertainment satisfaction. It gives them something to reflect upon as the lights come up in the theater.

The same elements usually found in the last act of a feature should be found in a short film: **Revelation**, **climax** and **resolution**. Climax and resolution are terms connected specifically to the outcome of the conflict and the ending of the story. Revelation, on the other hand, is not as concrete. Though all great films and fiction employ story revelation, the level of importance and degree of insight can vary dramatically. In this chapter, we examine all of these elements and their contribution to the overall effectiveness of a film.

Story Revelation— Character Revelation

Revelation means an element revealed or exposed (especially a striking disclosure) of something not previously known or realized. In great films, and all great fiction, there is a moment when crucial information cannot be concealed or withheld from the characters and the audience any longer. This information often is a shock, but it always makes sense. Often, it relates to motivations and/or backstory shedding light on one of the main characters and explaining what's going on in the story. Sometimes, it is a sudden realization or epiphany the protagonist has about her life as a result of the events experienced in the film. Sometimes, it is a realization or insight the audience has about the protagonist of which she remains ignorant.

In film and theater, this is the revelatory scene, the moment when the writer chooses to let the audience in on the motivation behind the characters and the story. The revelatory scene is one scene or a group of scenes where the truth is finally forced out into the open, and the characters, especially the protagonist, must cope with it. Now, we, the audience, understand why certain actions were taken despite the risks, and we realize what the film is really about.

In film, fiction and theater, **story revelation** is most often character revelation. Usually, it takes place during the second half of the work. In feature films and theater, the main revelation often occurs near the climax of the second act, although it can come as early as the end of the first act. (*Witness* has a shocking revelation at the end of the first act, when the protagonist John Book discovers that his supervisor is part of the murder he is investigating.) Many action films or thrillers employ this technique and, wherever it comes, it acts as a catalyst to propel the plot into the next portion of the film.

The revelation almost always has consequences, frequently drastic. Sometimes the startling information causes the protagonist to doubt himself before he finds the strength to recommit to the goal and story. Or, the recognition of an overpowering truth confirms the protagonist's struggle, sending him and the film hurtling toward the conclusion. It is important to dramatize these responses because they allow the audience to glimpse the protagonist's true character.

In a short film, the main revelation can occur almost anywhere in the second half of the film. As in a feature, it is more powerful when linked with another element, like a **reversal** or **crisis**, **climax** or **resolution**. By definition, a revelation is a surprise. It aids in creating suspense and offers entertainment by giving crucial but unexpected answers to the characters and the audience. Revelations are most powerful when they are simple but powerful. Often the revelation is saved for the last possible moment of a short film, when it is used to drive home the story's point.

Revelation & Exposition

To be truly effective, the revelation must have a direct relationship to the main exposition of the film. The problem set up at the beginning, which the protagonist is trying to solve, must be connected to whatever is revealed that leads to his success or failure. In a sense, the revelation is the reason why the protagonist encounters his difficulties while trying to achieve his goal. Once the revelation occurs, it can free the protagonist to attain his goal, or allow him to meet his fate more consciously. Sometimes only the audience is allowed to know the revelation of the story.

Again, whether the protagonist understands the revelation, or whether the revelation is offered only as a device for the audience to sum up the depiction of the character, it can illustrate not just the solution to the dramatic problem, but why the problem took the form it did. In "Life Lessons," the film's final scene (at Lionel's exhibition) illustrates this principle perfectly. Lionel hires a new young, pretty art groupie as his assistant; Paulette has been forgotten. Lionel demonstrates, primarily for our benefit as opposed to his own conscious awakening, that Paulette was important for his art, not in a personal way, but to fuel his emotion which then moved him to create his art. She was useful because she was young and pretty and interested in art—just as this new assistant is.

Richard Price also clarifies the "why" of Lionel's dramatic problem in this scene. Why were there questions about his ability to open the show and to stay involved with Paulette? The answer is found in the way he treats women: They are always young and pretty; he does not need to know them, man to woman; rather, he uses them as emotional enzymes in his creative process. He encountered his problems with Paulette out of necessity. As a modern young woman, she obviously was going to rebel against a man who used her femininity as a means to his creativity. She objected to his refusal to engage her personally, to offer candid assessments of her work, to help her as a lover would help her. Lionel doesn't like women, but respects their power and needs it for his work. Biographies of Picasso have proclaimed the same ideas, but Price's screenplay dramatizes the same issues in 45 minutes of entertainment.

Does Lionel know himself well enough to be aware of how he treats women? Yes, he realizes his feelings about them in the scene when Paulette finally leaves him, but he stifles his observation with a painted hand over his mouth. In the film's final scene, however, it is his behavior, the ultimate proof in drama, that demonstrates what he feels, as he starts the cycle again with a new female factotum.

Exposition can continue until the end of the film because in each new scene, the writer essentially gives the audience new information by revealing and exposing certain facets of the characters and story. But the main revelation must be held until the time is ripe with dramatic possibilities. Since the writer has the details necessary for the protagonist and audience, he doesn't need to reveal them until the impact will be greatest or the audience truly needs them in order to follow the story. Withholding the revelation helps maintain suspense by keeping the audience guessing about what is really going on.

Major & Minor Revelations

Revelations are major if they cause the action to be dramatically different than if they had never surfaced. A major revelation about the protagonist or another major character affects the story by creating a sudden illumination for the audience. Information the protagonist is unaware of—about himself or another character or another situation which directly affects the plot line similarly—can cause a revelation for the hero and audience.

Minor revelations tell the audience about motivations; they may not be dramatic, but they contribute to our understanding of the story and gain sympathy or empathy for the characters. Since a good film always contains surprises, a few minor revelations should occur throughout it.

Revelation of Character

Revelation of character can proceed in a variety of ways. If information is hidden from the audience, it can then illuminate the character for better or worse when revealed.

119

In "Hills Like White Elephants," the real source of conflict between Ash and Davis (played by Melanie Griffith and James Woods) is not revealed until the film's midpoint, when it is learned that she is pregnant and he wants her to have an abortion.

Behavior is an effective way to illustrate the character's true being. In "Anna Of Milan," Anna continually says she wants to change, to run away from her life. Randall, meeting her in the daytime and, riding around in her Rolls Royce, questions her sincerity. Anna is adamant that she wants to change because, she says, "Inside me there is only a void, an endless void." She wants to fill that void with Randall.

In the midst of a little passionate petting while driving Anna's car, he forgets himself momentarily after her statement. He opens his eyes in time to see that he's about to hit a boy selling flowers on the roadside. He swerves, loses control of the Rolls and hits a parked truck. Anna's reaction is the revelation: She cares only about her car, calling Randall an imbecile! So what if he had have hit the boy? Shaken and angered, Randall withdraws across the road as Anna takes charge, flagging down a man in a Jaguar to help her. The revelation, or the point of the story, is that no matter what Anna says, she is what she is—a materialist without social conscience. She confuses spirituality with sexuality, blurring Randall's hope and vision of her.

The writers foreshadow her true character at the start, for her monologue delivered, as she drives to meet Randall, numbly recounts the obligations and appointments her social position assigns her until even we, the audience, have had enough! Of course she should want to change. But by hinting at her true nature during the drive, the revelation (the contrast between her words and actions) is more believable.

A protagonist's **self-revelation** is a powerful moment of any film. Here, the protagonist experiences an epiphany about himself, especially in relationship to the conflict.

Again, let's look at "Life Lessons." After the climax when

Paulette leaves, Lionel angrily continues painting, muttering to himself. "Chippies, chippies. Know why they call them that?" he growls. "Because they like to chip away at you, man. Take a little chip. That's your art form . . . that's your talent. Chip, chip, chip." Suddenly, he gasps. His hand covers his mouth, smearing paint on his face and beard. Here, in anger, he reveals his true feelings for Paulette (and women in general), and he shows us he is aware of them.

In "Hills Like White Elephants," Ash's revelation is the climax of the film. She knows their relationship is over, nothing will ever be the same, despite what Davis tells her. All is now inalterably changed. If she has the abortion he wants her to have, it will destroy her and her love for him. If she has the child, it will destroy him because he does not want it. It is a no-win situation that will kill the relationship.

In "The Man In The Brooks Brothers Shirt," the final moment of the film is saved for the protagonist's self-revelation. After realizing the relationship with Jerry will evaporate, she contemplates her life on the train back to New York. Her last line, the last line of the film, expresses her conclusions: "There has to be more to the future than Jerry Breen, executive lover . . . unless there's—less." This sums up her hope about her life and her fear, and is essentially what the story is about: A look at the modern woman and her new role in society.

Revelation saved exclusively for the audience can be forceful and effective. We see this kind of revelation more often in novels, short stories and short films. In feature-length comedies, we usually find revelations that are not shared by the characters, as one last comic or ironic twist to make the audience laugh.

In *Occurrence At Owl Creek*, the final revelation is shocking and dramatic. The man has escaped and reaches out for his beloved when something strange happens. Using a film technique developed by Slavko Vorkapich (images of identical action filmed at slightly different angles and distances) writer/director Robert Enrico slows and prevents the lovers from meeting, creating the effect of an uncrossable chasm between husband and wife. As his love is finally within reach, the man's expression changes to one of horror. His body stiffens and contorts and the film cuts back to his hanging. The revelation is the hangman's rope never broke. Our journey has not been with an escapee on the run to his beloved, but one of fantasy inside a condemned man's mind. This technique, which creates a dark and powerful conclusion, has been used in feature films as *Jacob's Ladder* and *The Last Temptation Of Christ*.

Revelation Through Conflict

In film, new information is best revealed in action and through conflict. Revelation, too, is most effective when actions dramatize it or conflict forces it into the open, and not in flashbacks or expository speeches. Think of the revelations we've discussed above as examples.

Beginning writers often use **flashbacks** as a way to show something from a character's past. A flashback must be essential to the whole structure and not be used simply as a means of exposition. If it is in the film merely to tell something visually and does not utilize conflict or action, it will be flat and boring, and stall the forward momentum of the screenplay.

The same is true regarding an **expository speech**. If the protagonist has changed or realized something important, the change must be dramatic. It is dull to hear a character say, "And then I realized . . ." If the realization is a true revelation for the character, its importance will create emotion. Discover the emotion and it will help shape the scene.

Remember, we are more interested in characters who don't tell everything, especially what is painful. Use conflict to force the matter into the open; it brings emotion into the situation, making a stronger scene. Emotion, or the lack of it, can make or break a scene.

Revelation, Action & the Climax

The important revelation of a film can be dramatized in the protagonist's final action which resolves the conflict. Action is always more compelling than words, and if it surprises the audience, it can provide a startling disclosure about the character. At the end of "The Wedding," from *The Gold of Naples*, Teresa, betrayed by her bridegroom and tricked into a loveless marriage, walks out. But as she heads into the night, alone, with only her sordid profession to fall back upon, she stops. What will she do? Will she return to prostitution or accept Don Niccola's arrangement? For a long, agonizing moment she waits and we wait with her. Ultimately, she returns to his home, deciding that the deal he offers is better than returning to her difficult life on the street.

The revelatory moment or scene is an important element of the overall structure of a successful film. Revelation confers meaning to the characters and the story, generally going back to what the story is about. If the revelation is ineffective, there are several questions to ask:

1. What is the story really about?
2. What interested you in this story at the start?
3. What is really motivating the protagonist?
4. What is the protagonist afraid of?
5. Is one of the main characters hiding something?

The answers to any of these questions can provide you with a clue for finding the revelation hidden in the character's motivations or yours for writing the story. These are important questions to ask because story revelation can be a powerful moment within a screenplay and film. Without one, a film might be full of flash, but it will lack substance.

The Climax

The moment when a film, play or work of fiction reaches its greatest intensity and resolves the conflict is the **climax**. It is the decisive point of the plot and the most meaningful in relationship to the conflict and theme. Here, not only should the problem be solved, but the premise or theme clarified. In the climax, the writer drives the point of the story home.

The climax is the key to dramatic unity, which is the culminating point for both conflict and theme. The climax determines the worth and meaning of everything that has preceded it—the decisions, actions, obstacles, complications, crises. If the climax lacks power, the theme or premise has not dictated the progression of the conflict toward it as the goal. Somewhere the meaning has become obscured to the writer. Simply put, the climax tells us <u>who</u> succeeds and <u>why</u> he succeeds, thus determining the ultimate meaning of the work.

The climax makes the theme concrete in terms of an event. By focusing the film's action upon a definite goal, which ends at this event, the climax creates an integrated movement. In this way, the climax becomes a reference point against which to test the validity of every element of the structure. If a scene is not developing or leading up to this conclusion, it needs to be reconsidered and reworked, or thrown away.

The climax is not necessarily the final scene, but it is the one in which the conflict reaches its final stage. A resolution often follows, but not always, especially in short films where a final resolution of falling action may detract from the character twist or sense of irony. For example, in *Occurrence At Owl Creek*, climax and resolution are one.

Though it is discussed as a point in the action, the climax is not limited to a single scene. Depending upon the story, the climax may be very sudden and abrupt or it may be a complex event combining many lines of action into several scenes.

In a film, the climax must be visual and visceral, not internal. Though it does not have to end in screams, shootouts or car chases, an ending that incorporates strong actions is more powerful and memorable than one which is restricted or confined. The protagonist's emotional response to the end of the conflict should be included in the climax because it keeps the drama in human terms and makes it more understandable and satisfying to the audience.

Unity in Terms of Climax

Synthesis between action and theme is best shown in the climax of the film. Let's look at "Life Lessons" again. Chapter Three gave us a good outline of the conflict that leads up to the climax of the film.

In the climax of "Life Lessons," we are back in Lionel's studio where he turns his confessed passion for Paulette into a wonderful, powerful painting session. Each time Paulette has spurned him, he has run to his canvas and now his obsession has pushed her to the breaking point. In her room, she turns her anger and frustration on herself by striking out at her own paintings. Lionel tries to stop her. "Don't do that," he says. "Are you trying to punish me?" he asks. Paulette is incredulous. "Am I punishing you?" she responds. "Am I punishing you?!"

Paulette's brother is coming for her and she is leaving. Lionel again says he loves her, he'll do anything for her, but the lines sound hollow at this point. He switches tact and asks her about her painting. Paulette responds: "Don't give me this shit about how real artists have no choice. What's here? Am I good? Will I ever be good?! Come on, right now." When he doesn't reply, she shouts: "Come on!"

Lionel's inability to answer is all she needs to resume packing. "I'm going home," she says. Lionel chokes out the only words he can find. "You're young yet." And when these don't get her attention, he declares his love for her once more.

"Love me?" she practically screams. "You just need me around. Sometimes I feel like a human sacrifice. I don't know. Maybe if I was as good as you I wouldn't care about anybody else either, but I'm not, so good-bye."

Paulette's recognition of the truth, what she has been wrestling with all along is revealed. She aspires to create good work, great work. This is what she values. She doesn't want to be just another mediocre painter. Of course, no one knows the future and if she gives up, she'll never know. But only Paulette can find her way through this crisis. Only Paulette can determine what path she should take.

Lionel takes it personally. "Oh, so I'm the monster," he says. Then he argues insipidly about her own self-image. When this fails, he changes course again.

"Okay, look, maybe it's me. No, it's me," he admits. "You know, I indulge. I indulge in love, I indulge in making my stuff and they feed off each other, you know, they come together at times, but—this is bad, this is selfish . . . So," he mutters huskily, ". . . maybe . . . I should try and be a nice person for you. Maybe the key to that is to try and stop. You know, just to stop painting. Maybe I should— yeah, I should stop painting and be a nice person for you. Now is that what you want me to do, huh?!"

Clearly, this is not what he wants. But Lionel's confession shows us that he has some awareness of himself and his actions.

"I don't give a damn what you do," Paulette responds. "My brother's a United States Marine and I can't take this anymore. Get out of here. Get out of here! I can't take this anymore!!" she screams as she physically drives him from her room.

Lionel, predictably, returns to his canvas and his painting. Paulette, her brother in the background, comes in to say good-bye. Again she watches Lionel paint, awed and moved. "You know something?" she says. "If just once you came by my room and said, 'Gee, Paulette, you're a terrible painter, why don't you get a job and enjoy—'"

Lionel cuts her off, spinning from his work. "Lemme tell you something. You think I just use people, I just wring 'em out. Well, you don't know anything about me. You don't know how involved I get or how far down I go. Hell, I was married four times since before you were born, so don't you tell me." He pauses, staring at her. "So don't tell me."

With nothing left to say, Paulette leaves. Lionel angrily continues painting. His strokes are fierce, harsh. There is no doubt he's upset. He mumbles to himself. "Chippies. You know why they call 'em that? Because they like to chip away at you, man. Take a little chip at your art form, at your talent. Chip, chip, chip . . . " Suddenly realizing what he has said, he clamps a pigment-tainted hand over his mouth and smears paint on his face in horror.

The main conflict is now over, the story problem solved. This is where the main story has been heading since the film's midpoint: Lionel has failed to convince Paulette to stay. It was only a matter of time until he, with his jealousy and lies, drove her away. But what else do these scenes tell us about the characters and the conflict we have been watching?

The scenes sum up who the characters are, building on what we've previously seen. Lionel admits he is selfish, that he can devour relationships and feed them to his creative gods. His offer to give up painting is nothing short of disingenuous, because he can't truly give it up. It is what he lives for; it's who he is. On the other hand, Paulette's insecurities have driven her to an emotional brink. She wants Lionel, in the capacity of Great Artist, to reassure her about her art. She wants him to tell her she is good, she will be successful, that she is not wasting her time. Art is sacred to both of them. This is what held them together in the beginning and what ultimately drives them apart. It is the only thing Lionel can't lie about, and the one thing Paulette truly values.

The second climactic scene hints at a darker aspect of Lionel's personality. He uses the derogatory term "chippie" to refer to Paulette. (This is slang for a promiscuous woman or delinquent girl; originally, a prostitute.) He defines the word his own way, but that he thinks it reveals to us, and to him, his feelings about Paulette and women in general, and it shocks him. Ultimately, when we put it all together we see that Lionel can't love another person. He is in love with art. For Lionel, art requires his whole passion. This may or may not be the *sine qua non* of a true master, as Paulette recognized ("Maybe if I was as good as you I wouldn't care about anybody else either," she says), but he has little left for real people. The only honest relationship Lionel has is with his work.

These two scenes provide a strong climax to the film. The characters' emotions, attitudes and actions force the conflict to culminate. The theme is finally spelled out through the conflict, though it's been hinted at all along. Looking back, every scene contributes to the inevitability of the ending. No scene feels out of place. Thus the climax feels satisfying.

The Resolution

The events that follow the climax comprise the **resolution**. This is sometimes referred to as the **falling action**. Whatever is not resolved at the climax, is explained here. The resolution usually sets the circumstances of the film's world as a result of the climax, fixing the fates of the main characters. The best resolution bestows one last revelation or insight into the characters or story. It comes in the last pages, and in a short film, it usually needs to be only one scene.

If we left "Life Lessons" at the end of the climax, Lionel's character might be open for wider interpretation and the point of the story would be less specific. After all, people say things in anger they don't entirely mean. But because the resolution takes us to Lionel's art show, which is a big success, we gain more information.

Here, Lionel meets the young artist at the bar serving drinks. From the looks they trade, we see that he is as captivated by her as she is infatuated by him. Impulsively, he offers her Paulette's job, promising room, board, salary and, of course, life lessons. Watching them interact, we sense that Lionel is about to start a new cycle with this beautiful, unsuspecting fan. Now, we know that Paulette was right when she said she felt like a human sacrifice.

Emotional relationships are the sacramental offering to Lionel's god, his creative process, and this new woman will become the next oblation for his artistic altar.

Exercises

The bulk of the work on any plot is in the middle section, but the effort pays off in the last few scenes. Therefore, these scenes must be considered carefully.

Again, let's start with some questions to help focus the work needed to be done.

1. Is there a story revelation you have withheld from the audience?
    a. Is it minor or major?
    b. Does it come sooner than the climax of the film? Is this revelation linked to the plot problem?
    c. Why the protagonist is in trouble?
    d. In a sense, is it the reason for the screenplay?
    e. If so, is it a worthy revelation, enough to support a whole film, or can it be made stronger?

2. How can the revelation be shown to maximize its dramatic impact? (Combining it with the action of the climax is one way. Revealing it in the resolution is another.)

3. Is the climax the peak emotional moment in the plot—where decisive action leads to a solution of the plot problem?
    a. If not, can it be strengthened?
    b. Is it the result of the orchestration of forces within the main crisis?
    c. Is the solution a surprise for the audience?
    d. What is "proved" in the climax? Does it support your theme?

4. Does the resolution grow naturally out of the climax?
    a. Will the audience feel satisfied that it ties up all the loose ends?
    b. Is one last insight into the story offered in it?

Again, using the answers, organize your material. Look for ways to strengthen the drama (increase the stakes) at or before the climax. At the climax, push the forces to resolve the issues. A satisfying resolution ties up the last threads of the story.

Continue your scene outline, allotting two to five scenes to finish up the outline.

Once you have a full outline, set it aside. Before you return to it, review this chapter, as well as Chapters Three, Five and Six, especially the questions at the end of each one. Is the plot as original as it can be? Is it surprising as well as forceful? Are the characters pushing the action, the plot, as a result of who they are? (If not, return to Chapter Two and the questions at the end of it for help.)

As you go over your outline, look for ways to tighten it. If you have a beginning that is two or three scenes too long, rethink it now. Look, too, for ways to increase the visual conflict. A picture is worth a thousand words, and should your screenplay make it to the screen, it will be greatly enhanced by how well the story is told visually, through action. Make sure the forces push against each other hard enough to drive that action.

Once you are satisfied with your scene outline, you are ready for the fun part: Writing the actual screenplay.

PART THREE

The Structure
Of Scenes

8

CONSTRUCTING THE SCENE

Writing a **scene** is considered the fun part of screenwriting, the reward after all the hard work of creating characters and plot. Here, the characters and story come alive and the screenwriter's vision is realized. It's not unusual for many writers, itching to get started on the screenplay, to contemplate skipping over the preliminary steps and begin scripting without a complete outline. They plan on working out the characters and the plot during individual scenes.

There is no set formula for writing a screenplay. It is a mercurial process and everyone must find her own best method of working. But jumping into a scene before the characters and plot are sufficiently fleshed out can spell disaster for the beginning screenwriter. **Scenes** are structured action, each one advancing the development of the drama and our knowledge of the characters. Scenes are interconnected pieces of a greater whole, links in the progression of a story. Having an overview of the complete plot, and the relationships that make it work, gives cohesion to a first draft that might otherwise be missing. No matter how good a scene is, if it doesn't relate to those before and after, it cannot be considered successful in the context of the screenplay. (In interviews with writers, directors and actors you will often read how a wonderful scene was dropped because it just did not serve the story.) If the writer does not adequately understand a character or the point of a scene, she cannot do it justice.

Writing a great scene is an art and takes lots of practice. As in any art, there are principles of composition, techniques for construction and a craft for execution. In this chapter, we define the parameters of a scene, examine the principles behind its construction and reveal techniques to enhance the realization of the basic building block of drama.

Units of Action

A scene is a **unit of action**, a single event or exchange between characters, with unity of time and place. Screenplays are constructed from scenes which propel the plot forward, building to and falling from a story climax. A **plot** can be thought of as the blueprint from which a film is designed; scenes are the basic building blocks and the theme is the mortar that holds everything together. The scenes themselves should fit together so closely, and "match" the plot in your original specifications so well, that little glue is needed to insure the stability of the structure.

The organization of scenes makes the plot, which moves the story. As we have seen, the plot is the path the protagonist takes as he moves through the scenes toward his goal—all the time in conflict with the antagonist. Plot is structured—not random—action. Individual scenes are structured action, too.

Throughout this book, we use **action** in several capacities; e.g., the **rising action** of the middle, the **driving ac-**

tion of the screenplay. The action of a scene shares many ideas with these other uses of the term. Obviously, action is movement. In theater and literature, "the action" means the main subject or main conflict of a story, as distinguished from an incidental episode. "The action" also refers to an incident, event or series of events that make up the plot. The unfolding of the events in drama, according to the *Concise Dictionary of Literary Terms*, supplies an answer to the question, "What happens?" The dictionary continues its definition: "What characters say, do, and think and what results from their saying, doing, and thinking constitute the action of all narrative literature. A planned series of related and interrelated actions, which may be physical or mental or both, is said to make up the plot of a work of fiction or drama." A scene illustrates what characters say and do and the results of what they say and do.

The action of a scene must accomplish at least one of three goals:

1. Advance the flow of events (the plot) toward its inevitable conclusion (climax and resolution);

2. Advance the audience's understanding of the main characters by illuminating them through their behavior;

3. Advance the audience's understanding of the overall story by providing expository information.

Scenes are stronger when they utilize a combination of the first two goals. As we saw in Chapter Five, providing expository information can be an awkward task. Adding conflict or physical movement to an expository scene strengthens it. Combining exposition with either of the first two goals of a scene makes it stronger still.

When the scene is properly conceived, all three scene goals relate to a film's plot directly or indirectly. We dramatize a story by showing our characters probing, investigating, and interacting with other forces in the film; the plot grows out of these actions. Showing something im-

135

portant that leads to a better understanding of a character and her motivation relates indirectly to the plot; the audience needs to understand or intuit motivations in order to make sense of the overall story. Finally, exposition is crucial to the plot since, by definition, the information is vital to the audience understanding the conflict or characters. Without the appropriate exposition, audiences will not be properly oriented to the film. (See Chapters Three and Five.) If too many scenes fail to achieve one or more of these goals, the plot structure will crumble.

The Principles of Construction

Above, we discussed a scene as a unit of action that advances the plot. Scene action is the movement within the scene. For example, a character starts at a definite place or with a definite understanding of the dramatic situation; at the end of the scene, that character or another is in a slightly different place or has furthered his understanding of the conflict. Whichever it is, by the end of the scene, something has been altered.

Theater Scenes vs. Film Scenes

In the theater, the proscenium separates the audience from the play. The audience will accept many theatrical conventions and contrivances, but a play succeeds primarily for two reasons. First, because the spoken word moves the audience, and second, depending upon the relationship established between the actors and the audience, the experience is immediate and powerful.

In a movie, the camera sits in place of the audience. Anywhere the camera can fit offers the audience a view of the action it does not otherwise get from a theater seat. For example, the camera can place the viewer inside a malfunctioning space capsule thousands of miles from earth, in the eye of a tornado, or in the face of raw emotion. It can create a sense of freedom with wide open spaces or a feeling of claustrophobia. The camera can record several characters' reactions to a brutal incident by the use of the close-up. It can transcend geography by cutting from continent to continent in seconds. Because most films strive for realism, the camera's close proximity to the drama increases the viewer's involvement. A successful film performance then, can be infinitely more intense and visceral than a theater experience because it can take you right into the heart of the drama. As a result, films, unlike plays and sitcoms, are not always made up of fully developed scenes, because films have both more freedom and more limitation.

But the freedom to move anywhere the production budget permits also creates certain limitations. No matter how interesting a scene is, it cannot play on and on if it does not perform any of the scene functions described above, or if it does not conform to the theme. The average length of a scene in a short film is about one to four pages, although some will be longer and some shorter. What's important is that any scene fit the rhythm of the whole film.

We expect films to rely more heavily on visuals whereas plays and sitcoms are allowed wide latitude with dialogue. A filmmaker is not limited only to the visual, however; what characters say and how they say it is also important. But the filmmaker's use of his materials—space, time, color, light and sound—creates and defines the film's world. The visual and aural quality of the medium (space, color, light and sound) and its plasticity (time) can create the appearance of reality or even hyper-reality. Theater scenery and props can only suggest reality. As film characters move through space and time, illuminated to appear saintly or satanic, they conjure specific visual images and create the audience's experience. The more powerful these images, the greater the impact on the viewer because they appear so real and so close. Although a screenplay is more a blueprint than a completed structure, it should provide the inspiration for powerful imagery in order to successfully move the composition from the storyboard to production.

One Main Point Per Scene

Every good scene has **one main point** the writer wants to communicate. The point of a scene can be an incident or event in the development of the plot or an aspect of the character's motivations. Sometimes the main point is to make the audience feel something or to empathize with a character. The scene might dramatize the emotional impact of the preceding actions on a main character or show the results of a character's earlier efforts to achieve his goal.

Presenting too many points in one scene will create problems for the audience. They will not know what to pay attention to, and lose track of the story progression. Other ideas may be addressed in the scene, and often should be, but they must complement— and not obscure— the main issue.

If too many scenes combine ideas of equal importance, the audience will become confused or lose interest because the film will seem unfocused. A good solution to this problem is to create separate scenes for each equally important point. Even if the characters simply walk from inside to outside in one continuous movement, separating the important ideas between different locations will help focus the points. "Life Lessons" is a good example: After Lionel critiques Paulette's work, telling her that art is about "having to do it," he walks away from her, critical of himself and the way he sounded.

Visual Actions

It is the screenwriter's job to consider what is visually interesting and exciting in a scene. Showing characters in movement, physically doing interesting things, is more dynamic than actors talking on the stage or television. The rule is: "Don't talk about it, show it!"

Throughout "Life Lessons," Lionel responds to Paulette's denial of him by painting. He doesn't tell us he is going to paint, he simply assaults his canvas. We watch him passionately slap and smear color around until his painting metamorphoses into a brilliant masterpiece. Because we see the actions for ourselves instead of hearing about them, Lionel's action has greater significance.

Dramatizing a story through the characters' actions instead of through dialogue deepens the audience's involvement. When we watch characters struggle to achieve their goals, it involves us in an active process. We wonder: "Will they succeed?" This is a more emotional question than, "what is the importance of what he is telling me with his dialogue now?" When characters act more and talk less in a scene, the audience must interpret those actions. For an effective interpretation, the writer must provide hints to the actual motivations. It is this active participation that makes viewers more deeply feel for and identify with the characters. But when characters tell too much about themselves or the story, audiences will tune them out or disbelieve them.

"The Dutch Master" illustrates the effectiveness of character <u>action</u> rather than dialogue. Various narrators and commentators relate Teresa's story, but it is Teresa's actions which intrigue us most because we watch as she becomes captivated by the painting. We observe as she searches for something more than what awaits her in marriage. When the painting comes to life, we see her shock. And when the Dutchman "invites" her into the scene, we know she will go, and we travel with her, willingly. Teresa never says a word, but as we watch her actions we have a better understanding of her than her closest friends, and we are more interested in her precisely because there is yet so much to know. It is the contrast between what the other characters say and the reality of what we see that helps keep up our interest in the film. Why does the painting so fascinate her? What is happening to her? What do all her actions mean? These questions are left to the audience to sort out, after the film is over.

Where a scene takes place greatly affects its **mood**. An open field at dawn, midday or sunset, during summer, winter, spring or fall yields different interpretations. A study of Impressionist Claude Monet's paintings of grain stacks at different times and seasons demonstrates the effect of light on mood.

The execution that begins *Occurrence At Owl Creek* takes place at sunrise. The murky images of the battle-scarred landscape in the predawn light cast a desolate pall over the setting and establish a sense of foreboding. As the hangman slips the noose over the condemned man's head, the feeling of dread intensifies.

Of course, before there is a visual, words must describe it. Words are the screenwriter's first and only tools. Unlike all other steps in the production of a film, writing the screenplay is conveying the imagination in words. The closer the words describing the images and characters' actions are to conveying the power, excitement and passion a viewer feels watching the completed film, the more successful the screenplay will be.

Scene Progression

Just as action in a screenplay builds to the most dramatic point (the climax) the movement within a scene must build from the least important idea to the most. If the significant point is given at the beginning of the scene, all the action that follows will be anticlimactic. So, instead of growth, amplification or development, there will be a letdown for the audience. Once the main point is made, the scene should be over.

Every good scene has a point when the substance or action of the scene begins. This is sometimes referred to as the "**button**." A few lines of dialogue or a few seconds of visuals may setup the scene, but once hit, the action (struggle or conflict of the scene) starts. A button functions like the inciting incident in a plot: it gets things moving. It occurs within a few seconds of the scene's opening and sends the line of action toward the main point.

From the scene's introduction, a progression builds to what the point of the scene is: a plot development, character revelation or sometimes just a funny line after a piece of exposition.

The middle section usually shows the struggle or conflict involved as the main character (in the scene) attempts to achieve something important. The flow of the scene may appear to head in one direction and then as a result of new information or a surprise response, it may suddenly veer off on a new course, similar to the plot line of a screenplay. The action is always headed toward the climax of the scene.

Beginning and ending a scene are sometimes the most difficult part of its creation. Where it begins or ends does not usually coincide with an entrance or exit. The beginning of a scene might be built into the previous one. The same is true of a scene's end, which can be built into the scene following it. In "Life Lessons," the beginning of a street scene showing Lionel and Paulette on their way to a party really occurred in the prior scene when the two were dressing for the affair. At the midpoint of "Life Lessons," Paulette is leaving New York and Lionel. In this scene, she tries to confront him, but he is lost in his painting. Unable to rouse him, she watches him paint and we watch her anger dissolve. The next scene shows Paulette getting ready to go to a party with Lionel. Clearly, at some time between the two scenes, she changed her mind. We were not told at the end of the first scene what her decision was. We are simply shown it in the context of the next scene, and this makes the moment more meaningful.

Sequences

Using more than one scene to illustrate a focused action, like Paulette's decision to stay in New York, is an example of a **scene sequence**, which is a group of scenes built around a single idea, incident or event in which the locations change but the focus of the action remains the same. The group of party scenes in "Life Lessons" builds to the moment when Lionel forces Paulette to retaliate viciously; she leaves with another man. In the following scene, we see she has taken the man back to the studio, to her bed, right under Lionel's nose.

Often, whole sections of short films are built by grouping scenes around the development of a single idea that shows its progression. A look at the structure of the scenes in "Life Lessons," *Occurrence At Owl Creek*, "The Dutch Master," *Peel*, "Mara Of Rome," "The Wedding," "Hills Like White Elephants" illustrates this. Short films usually stay closer to the characters than do features, which often seem to prefer hardware in action sequences (car chases, alien invasions, etc.) over characterization. In short films, the scenes are used to show the development of motivations, decisions and actions, and their consequences. If these motivations, decisions and actions are sufficiently dramatic, i.e., noteworthy, moving and vivid, they can draw the audience into the film just as effectively, sometimes even more so, than special effects.

A scene sequence in a short film is a way to avoid an overly episodic or incidental feel to your story. Characters reveal themselves slowly over a number of scenes, which adds suspense to the delineation of their character arcs. Indeed, many short films consist of a single-scene sequence ending when we have learned what we need to know about the characters. Think back to *The Lunch Date*.

Techniques for Construction

Writing a great scene is a special talent, like having an ear for funny dialogue. Some screenwriters are more naturally inventive and skillful than others. Still, few scenes come into being fully formed. Good scenes are the product of careful planning, hard work, and reworking; successful screenwriters tend to utilize particular techniques when composing their scenes. Discovering these techniques can save the beginning screenwriter lots of time and anguish.

Starting Off

Before writing a scene, spend a little time thinking about it. Clarify the topic and main point for yourself. You need to know:

1. Who is in the scene?
2. Where will it play?
3. What do the characters want in the scene?
4. What do they need (the subtext) in the scene?
5. What are their attitudes?
6. Where is the conflict or tension coming from?

Clearly, the answers to Questions 1 and 2 are self-evident. But the screenwriter must get beyond the obvious. Often, first thoughts and choices about a scene are familiar or, worse, clichéd. So it's important to take time to examine a number of questions at the onset. Not only must you know who is in the scene and where it takes place, but what the relationships are between the characters. For example, husbands and wives, siblings, employer and employee, all may have varying relationships depending on their backstories or earlier scenes in the film. Not all husbands and wives are loving, and not all employers and employees play opposite each other in the same way. If they do, it's usually boring. Additional characters in a scene, other than the primary participants, can lend values not readily apparent: main characters can play off minor characters for comedic or dramatic purposes; minor characters can provide a counterpoint to the main characters, or reinforce them.

Setting, too, can add or detract from a scene. As we have noted above, a scene's locale, including time, season and weather, contributes to creating and maintaining atmosphere. But there are far more important reasons to consider location. The skilled screenwriter often takes advantage of what's available in the setting for the characters to relate to and use. Giving the characters scenery to connect with or physical props to put into their hands, enlivens a scene and increases its level of reality. In *Peel*, the orange is a terrific prop, not only to escalate the drama but for the rhythm and punctuation it provides before the viewer realizes its importance. Lionel's studio and loft in "Life Lessons" provide a rich setting; props abound to be exploited.

Beginning writers often don't give enough thought to the settings for their scenes. They sometimes use the first locale that occurs to them. But setting can add color to screenplays; it can enhance dramatic value by offering characters opportunities to perform revealing actions; it can reflect their emotions. It is always worthwhile to consider exactly where a scene should play in order to maximize the location's contribution to the overall screenplay.

Goals & Objectives

Every film needs a protagonist who has a goal, because the goal directs the film. Will Lionel convince Paulette to stay? Will the condemned man escape? Will Anna sleep with Randall? The plot must stay focused on its story goal.

In every scene the characters have **scene goals** or **scene objectives**. (Actors often write very good scenes because they understand this need from scene work.) Scene objectives do not have to be exactly the same as the overall **story goal**. If it is a scene goal, it is generally connected to the character's desire. If it is a scene objective, it may be related to the character's need, i.e., the protagonist may want specific information to aid him in his pursuit of his goal. The information is not the goal, it is connected to it. A writer sometimes offers a scene to show how a particular action or piece of information has affected a character. As a result, the character may need comfort or prodding. These scenes strengthen and deepen characterization.

A scene's important characters often have conflicting desires. The protagonist often conflicts with others besides the antagonist. These other characters provide obstacles or complications for the protagonist to overcome. In "Life

Lessons," the opening scene illustrates this point. Philip wants to enter the studio and see Lionel's paintings for the upcoming show. Lionel doesn't want Philip to see his work. They both have concrete goals. Lionel controls the elevator and keeps the man out. While they are in conflict, exposition for the story is divulged without anyone suspecting a thing.

As discussed in Chapter Two, characters' conscious wants often conflict with their unconscious needs. It's important to figure out if this is a source of conflict that can add dimension to a scene. In *Peel*, the father says he wants his son to pick up all the orange peel thrown on the highway; what the father needs is to address his anger at his sister. He doesn't satisfy his need and his son runs off, creating more conflict between the father and his sister. "Anna Of Milan" portrays this type of conflict, too. At the beginning, Anna says she is ready for change; we see that she wants Randall. To her, he represents change. But as the story points out, she is incapable of change. What she needs is power, to feel in control, which is probably the reason this married woman has affairs. In a number of scenes, the discrepancy between her want and her need comes into play.

Scene Subtext

What the character needs in a scene usually relates to the **subtext**, what is going on beneath the surface words and actions. This is such an important element to understand that Chapter Ten will deal with it exclusively.

Sometimes the tension in a scene comes from what precedes it. All of Lionel's painting scenes in "Life Lessons" work well because they result from and show his response to the conflict with Paulette. "Quiet" or "happy" scenes in your story should be included only as long as the conflict is kept hanging over the characters' heads and the audience aware of it. It is paramount that the characters not escape the problem until it is solved.

The characters' **attitudes** can bring added tension or

humor to a scene, depending on what happened to the characters before the scene. The cause of these attitudes does not have to be shown. Sometimes it is enough to drop in a line of dialogue to explain what's motivating the behavior. In the first scene of *Peel*, the father and his sister's attitudes are built upon what has happened previous to the film's opening. An impending action also might influence the behavior of a character, for good or bad. A character late for a meeting might have a different attitude than one on his way to his own wedding.

Think Visually

As you approach a scene, you always must keep in mind how it is going to look. Think visually about the scene and the film. As the scene is written, try to see it in your mind's eye. What does the setting look like? What is on hand for the characters to use that will make the scene more interesting and more real? Always try to find meaningful actions for the characters and audience. Mentally picture the action, then think, "If I didn't have dialogue, how would I communicate the important idea of the scene?"

Another question to ask is, "How have I seen this type of scene done before?" Determining this before writing can save time and aggravation by eliminating clichés and unconscious imitations. Try to be as original as possible. Originality and inventiveness surprise the audience and make better films than the stale and predictable. How many ways can a love scene play under a harvest moon? Ask, "How I can do it differently?"

Business

In a scene, the personal actions of a character are referred to as **business**. These specific actions (e.g., pouring a drink, eating an apple, fixing a meal) include anything people occupy themselves with while alone or interacting with others.

Business contributes a number of valuable functions to the overall effectiveness of a film. Day-to-day activities help

146

create a sense of reality on the screen. Seldom do people sit in head-to-head dialogue except in very specific situations. (Even in confessionals and psychiatrists' offices, we are distracted by the grate of the screen or a painting on the wall.) Most of the time, we are engaged in routine activities while talking with others. Routine actions also lend physical movement to scenes and keep them from becoming static. Since you want to **think visually**, keeping the characters' business in mind will help you.

A scene that specifically includes business which suits the character helps define who that character is and gives the audience clues about his total personality. We all know that actions speak louder than words, and audiences tend to give greater credence to what they see as opposed to what they hear. A woman who putters at jigsaw puzzles, opposed to one who goes on wild shopping sprees create different comments about their respective personalities.

Because of the strong influence actions make on assessing characters, business should not be considered incidental or just movement. Business reinforces the characterizations. If a character's business contradicts his dialogue, the scene can make a much stronger impression than a speech that tells the audience exactly what the character is thinking. If a character wants to hide his emotions but the writer wants the audience to understand and empathize with him, business can provide the telling actions. Although dialogue is extremely convenient for expressing inner thoughts and feelings, it often undermines the power of the character and the scene in which it tells us too much. More on this appears in Chapter Ten.

Humor

Anywhere **humor** fits naturally into a screenplay, a writer should consider using it, regardless of genre. Humor should be organic to the situation in the scene, and should not be inserted as an excuse to be funny. Unlike some feature films, most short screenplays are better served by funny characterization and situations than by funny dialogue or quips. Jokes which turn the protagonist into a stand-up comedian tend not to advance the action, but rather slow the story down. Effective comedy isn't based on wisecracks or mechanical gimmicks. The banana peel isn't funny, it's the character who slips on it that gets you the laugh.

Even the darkest tragedies benefit from a little **comic relief**. In a serious or tragic work, the writer purposely uses a humorous scene, incident or remark to relieve emotional intensity and, simultaneously, to heighten the seriousness or tragic implications of the action. Shakespeare illustrates this with the humor found in *Hamlet*. And what would *Romeo and Juliet* be without Mercutio's humorous observances? Even in *Macbeth*, the drunken porter provides much-needed comic relief to the dark portent of the tale.

Humor, of course, can be broad or realistic, light or heavy-handed, it all depends upon your story. In "Life Lessons," Richard Price uses humor to lighten an otherwise serious tale. Early in the film, Lionel shoots a basketball in his studio. His basket is next to the window into Paulette's bedroom. After making several shots, he fires one off that goes through Paulette's window, drawing an angry response from her and a laugh from us.

In *Ray's Male Heterosexual Dance Hall*, much of the humor comes from the dialogue, which contrasts Sam's thoughts with his actions.

Filmmakers David Lean and Ronald Neame were partnered on several films early in their careers. Mr. Neame is fond of saying that after he and Mr. Lean knew the point and the conflict of a scene, the last thing they would do is see if humor could fit into the scene organically. After all, films are entertainment.

Economy

It is an unwritten law that films always must move ahead: Every scene must advance the action, every line must keep sight of the climax. Description and dialogue must be as focused as every other element in a screenplay. Random descriptions of every detail in a scene will only derail the script. Usually, when setting a scene, the slugline provides the implied detail, for example:

INT. ARTIST'S STUDIO—DAY

A line or two of description, noting numerous blank canvases scattered around the large room or an expensive bottle of cognac lying amidst paint brushes, will tell the reader enough to get the picture. Descriptions should always be kept to a minimum.

Another way to keep screenplays lean is to enter the scene at the latest possible moment. A scene that opens with a relevant plot topic dispenses with boring or superfluous material. As soon as the scene's goal is accomplished, it should end. Stay away from entrances, exits and introductions. These take up time and contribute little to the film.

Exercises

Take a scene that you know well from your plot outline and write it. Go over it a few times in the next few days until you feel good about it. Set it aside for a week, then return and analyze it. (This exercise also will work by using a scene from a produced screenplay.)

1. Locate the main point of the scene. What is it trying to accomplish? Is it telling us about character or conveying a plot point? Is it clear?

2. What is visually interesting in the scene? What business are the characters engaged in to enhance the visual quality of the story? What is the mood?

3. What do the main characters want in the scene? What do they need? What are their attitudes? What are their scene objectives? Isolate the conflict.

4. How does the scene progress? Is there a specific moment where the scene takes off (hits the "button")? Is it close to the beginning of the scene or does it come later? Are there surprises in the scene? Is the scene emotional? Does it make its point and end?

5. What do we learn about the characters from dialogue and from visuals? Characterize how the scene shifts from beginning to end in terms of the relationships.

6. What is the subtext of the scene? Is there anything going on beneath the surface dialogue? If not, can the scene be improved by adding subtext?

Return to the scene using what you've learned and rewrite it. Save it for the exercises at the end of the next chapter.

9

DIALOGUE:
THE SEARCH FOR
THE PERFECT LINE

The last chapter discussed many aspects of scene construction except for the most obvious: **dialogue**. Because dialogue is one of the two most prominent elements of a screenplay, it requires its own chapter to fully cover its scope. In drama or literature, we think of dialogue as conversation between characters. But in any fictional medium, dialogue is not conversation; it is the illusion of conversation. Real conversation is random, repetitive and often pointless while dramatic dialogue is ordered and purposeful.

Writing good dialogue, terrific dialogue, is like writing a great scene. It takes lots of practice. Some screenwriters have a natural gift for turning a phrase, using humor or innuendo to deepen the meaning. A dedicated student, though, can go a long way with hard work. He can learn to actively listen to the different patterns of speech people use and develop an ear for words. Taking notes of particularly prime exchanges is another way a novice writer can grow. This chapter defines the main function of dialogue in a visual medium, examines what makes it good, and presents certain techniques to aid the beginning screenwriter in his pursuit of the perfect line.

The Function of Dialogue

The role of dialogue in a screenplay is to:

1. Advance the plot toward its climax;
2. Advance the audience's understanding of the main characters;
3. Advance the audience's understanding of the story by providing information which can't be shown;
4. Set the tone for the film (especially in comedy).

Film dialogue must be crafted within the context of character and conflict. It must give the appearance that it is what a specific character would say under a specific set of circumstances. Yet, it cannot stray too far from the main topic of the screenplay. If a line does not serve one of these basic functions, the writer should consider cutting it from the page.

Advancing The Plot

The plots of films, plays and novels grow out of the interaction between conflicting characters. These exchanges between characters always involve dialogue, which generally makes up the largest portion of a scene as well as the screenplay. When dialogue helps advance the plot, it relates directly to the conflict. This doesn't mean that the dialogue only describes specific plot-oriented details, but it helps illustrate the progress of the conflict by showing how the conflict affects the characters and what they do as a result.

Almost every scene in "Life Lessons" advances the conflict, and the dialogue reflects this. From the moment Lionel picks up Paulette at the airport until she walks out of the studio, he struggles verbally with her, trying to rekindle their relationship only to further alienate her. The only time the plot conflict takes a back seat is just after the midpoint, when Paulette has changed her mind about leaving. As the two get ready for a party, they act and speak like an old married couple. The few scenes showing them on their way to and eventually arriving at the party are used to reveal Lionel's character, but by then, the conflict is already locked in place and the film can afford a short breather.

Revealing Character

What characters say and what they don't say are primary ways they reveal and define themselves. How a person speaks can be very telling about where she comes from, her level of education, and so on. Her diction or choice of words provide hints to her deeper nature. Dialogue should be thought of as a function of character. Within the context of film unity, it is an action—not merely a device—to tell the story. Dialogue allows the audience to more specifically comprehend the character and distinguish her from others.

Physical action is considered the best revelation of character in a film, but sometimes only dialogue can expose real character motivations. Such dialogue should always be considered carefully. If a speech is too precise in its description of past events, it will ring false and lose impact because in real life these disclosures are rarely made, and then usually under stress. A film character should face extraordinary circumstances when something compels him to drop his guard and reveal himself or his innermost feelings. When character revelation of this sort is properly motivated, it provides a powerful comment on the character—all the more so when it portrays him in a radically different light from what the audience expects.

Providing Information

Chapter Five already described the nature and importance of expository information. Generally, dialogue plays a part in conveying the main exposition. But as a film progresses, additional information is needed. Characters make discoveries about each other or about their dramatic situations. Many of these discoveries are visual, but most often they need confirmation and elucidation through dialogue.

Information given in dialogue must be consequential to the story or characters. If the audience does not need to know it to understand the elements, don't offer it.

Setting the Tone

When dialogue helps set the tone of a film, it is usually in a comedy. A sense of foreboding or catastrophe is best achieved through visuals and drama, not through poetic or overly dramatic dialogue, while comedy relies on humor, funny lines, jokes and gags, both visual and verbal. When dialogue crackles with quips and jokes, audiences respond with laughter; it can effectively establish a film's tone in seconds.

The Characteristics of Good Dialogue

Again, dialogue is not real conversation, but the illusion of it. As anyone knows who has read a court transcript or taped a college class, the best dialogue is not an edited version of real speech; it is invention, contrived conversation that satisfies the demands of its scene. But it must sound real to work. If dialogue sounds stilted, false, corny, or clichéd, it can destroy a worthy story.

In a feature or a short film, dialogue has the same characteristics. It is at its best when it differentiates characters, when it is clear, when it advances the tension in a scene, when it is to the point, but not "on the nose."

Voice

A character's individual voice is one of the most important ways he reveals himself. Voice is more than just how a character talks. It reflects where he has come from and where he has gone. It gives an indication of how he thinks, what's important to him and what's not, and to some degree, of psychology.

In Chapter Two, we mentioned that a character's birthplace will influence who he will become. His behavior will differ if he is born in Scarsdale rather than the South Bronx. Patterns of speech show where a person comes from, as do accents and dialects. Certain phrases and expressions are particular to specific ethnic backgrounds and classes. Good grammar (or bad) usually clues us in to someone's education. The use of special jargon characterizes occupations, and slang often identifies time and place. Understanding and using the special way people talk brings dialogue to life, making it colorful and real.

Through dialogue, a writer illustrates differences between people. One can be philosophical or literal, make allusions or be direct. For example, the owner of a racehorse usually speaks differently than the stable hand who grooms it. Even characters of similar backgrounds often have different speech patterns, depending on their interests and their philosophies. A sense of humor defines one character while the lack of one defines another.

Emotion often forces people to revive patterns of speech they believe they have left behind. A woman who moved from Brooklyn and tried to leave every trace of it behind, may find that her accent returns at the worst possible moment—when angered, for example.

To understand how different people speak, a writer needs to develop an ear for words. As long as a writer works within his own scope, dialogue should not be a problem. But when characters are introduced with backgrounds divergent from his, research becomes a true ally. **Research** lends authenticity to a plot and milieu, and it also often produces a colorful and esoteric language which gives any screenplay authority and reality.

A look at two films, both set in New York illustrates this point. "Life Lessons" deals with educated, artistic individuals and their dialogue in the film reflects this. In "The Dutch Master," except for Dr. Roserman and the museum docent, all characters are working-class and sound like it.

Simplicity

In a film, dialogue needs to be understood the first time it is heard. You can't rerun a passage in a film, taking time to think about it, the way you can reread a book. The audience is listening to the dialogue and has to grasp its meaning before the film moves ahead. Therefore, the best dialogue is usually simple, coming in short, ordered sentences that give the illusion of real speech.

In real life, people tend to talk in short sentences or in sentence fragments, with simple, direct words. They interrupt each other, repeat, and overlap. Effective dialogue, however, cannot use the same patterns, because it will lose momentum and power. The writer, though, can sparingly use interruptions and repetitions to emphasize what a character is saying and to show another's reaction, thus adding to the appearance of reality. However, reality can't always be the guide. For example, overlapping dialogue, though realistic, should be avoided unless there are specific reasons for it.

Poetic, flashy, and complex words and sentences generally confuse the dialogue's meaning, making it hard to follow, whether listening or reading. This doesn't mean that poetry or flashy phrases shouldn't be used, or that complex thoughts or esoteric language should never be expressed. A character distinguished by verbal cunning or abstract logic would in fact, use this type of language.

Progression

Just as a scene progresses to its most dramatic point, so should dialogue. Lines must build from the least significant to the most in order to develop the innate tension such **progression** contains. Whether the speech is dramatic or comedic, the principle is the same.

In comedy, lines develop to the funny twist that makes you laugh, or, the punch line. Good writers save the joke until the end of a speech. If it comes at the beginning and the audience laughs, it can get in the way of or conceal important material that follows. Also, in comedy, jokes tend to need a line or two to set up. "It's not like I'm picky," the lady lawyer says. "All I want is a guy who's tall, dark—and has no prior felonies."

Always save the strongest lines for scene finales in order to maximize their impact.

Economy

Many screenplays depend too heavily upon dialogue to communicate every aspect of the story. Proportionately, short films tend to use even less dialogue than features. Film is a visual medium and dialogue need not tell the viewer what he will learn by watching the screen.

The best dialogue is lean. Brevity is more valuable than amplification in a screenplay, especially in dialogue. Because film is a visual medium, the shorter the film segment, the more its visual origins are stressed. Think of the best commercials for example, and how they emphasize the visuals, dialogue is then used at the end to underscore the message. Remember, behavior and deeds are stronger indicators of a person than his words. Extraneous words, lines and even whole speeches should be cut whenever possible. As long as clarity is not an issue, these cuts will only strengthen the dialogue, not weaken it.

Long speeches work better in novels and plays than in films. A screenwriter must have a good reason to include one. Any passage running more than four or five lines should be studied carefully for trimming or complete removal. **Monologues** are a theatrical device, not a filmic one. If a character uses a long speech to explain how something works, it slows the action. The writer needs to consider length and get the information across in a simpler way. However, a long speech used for the revelation of character is a different matter. **Self-revelation** can be very powerful. After all, this is sometimes the whole point of a film. In this case, the writer should take his time with the speech in order to maximize the impact of it on the audience.

"On-the-Nose" Dialogue

When dialogue is too direct or too clear, it often rings false, especially when speeches involve emotional issues. In real life, most people have difficulty expressing or communicating their emotions, tending to conceal or deny them. Others don't want to confront emotional issues and talk around them. Since film strives to capture the appearance of reality, real-life responses are most crucial when they involve issues that the audience can identify with. Emotion is a powerful universal element.

The heart of a great film is its emotional wallop. So emotion must be forced out into the open where the audience can identify with the characters feeling it. Often, beginning screenwriters will avoid emotion and conflict in their writing, or will be too obvious in their use. Both extremes can jeopardize whatever goodwill the audience may feel on behalf of the film.

The art of screenwriting is to capture characters' indirection so that audiences grasp the true, deeper meaning of what is happening until the moment the characters force each other to disclose their real motivations. When viewers make the associations for themselves, from their own lives and backgrounds, the characters' experiences take on greater significance, and so does the film. When characters imply, rather than state too obviously what they are feeling, the audience is able to make the associations and connect more deeply with the characters. In the next chapter, on subtext, we will discuss this in more detail.

"Life Lessons" illustrates how the dialogue revolves around important emotional issues. In the second scene, when Paulette gets off the jet and finds Lionel waiting for her, she doesn't tell us she is angry, her attitude and actions do. In the same scene, when Lionel learns of Paulette's weekend with another man, he doesn't say he's jealous, his behavior does. He acts hurt, then attacks the other man with sarcasm.

Techniques & Tips

To create dialogue that sounds natural and rolls effortlessly off the actor's tongue, there are a few techniques and tips that will assist the beginning writer.

Rough It Out

Once the formal idea for a scene is in mind and most (if not all), of the questions discussed in Chapter Eight have been answered satisfactorily, you are ready to begin writing. A good idea is to first rough out the scene without censoring any thoughts. It doesn't matter if the speeches are long and full, if they are too flowery, too direct, or too pedantic, or whether ideas are repeated and clichés abound. Sometimes the characters just have to speak in order for you to discover the heart of a scene.

Often, from these flabby speeches, one or two lines will be real gems and say everything necessary. Save these lines for the most significant places within the scene. Then, the rest of the speech can be red-penciled.

Now look, word by word, at the dialogue and the scene. Most of the speeches should be no longer than one or two lines. (Formatting is very important to determine the proper line length; see Appendix A.) Take out anything that sounds clichéd and look for better ways to express your ideas. Then, rewrite. Don't be afraid to juggle the beats of the scene around, using a piece of dialogue at the beginning that was originally written for the end. See what happens. Sometimes this will show that the whole first half of a scene is extraneous and can be dropped.

When the scene is finished, you're ready for the next step.

Read It Out Loud

<u>Always read your dialogue out loud</u>. The best indicator of how it sounds is by listening to how it rolls off your own tongue. Dialogue is written to be spoken; it must sound natural. The only way to hear if dialogue sounds natural is to listen to it carefully. If the words and sentences are awkward or hard to speak, then it is ineffective screenplay dialogue.

Reading the dialogue out loud will also help determine if your characters sound alike. You want to capture the different ways people talk; this is accomplished by utilizing different phrases or rhythms for different characters. One character might always use business jargon, even when away from his office. Another might always use simple, everyday speech, even when describing a complex medical emergency.

Depending upon how good an actor you are, speaking the dialogue aloud can also indicate whether or not emotion builds through a scene. Listening to your dialogue tells you if it moves to the most dramatic point, or jumps from one emotion to another. If it jumps from one emotional extreme to another, then the scene should be restructured to show a progression of emotion.

Nonverbal Language

Not all communication is verbal. In any scene, much can be relayed by the way a character looks at another, or through nonverbal reactions.

Remember, in film, the camera sits in place of the audience. By taking us right into the face of a character, it can show us—with a reaction—how someone feels without her uttering a word. Through the use of action, mood, music, editing, film can amplify small gestures which would be missed on stage. The majority of times, the action will be stronger than dialogue. However, the description of the outward appearance and quality of the action should be succinct. It is better to suggest and imply than to be absolute, because then the reader has an opportunity to fill in the blanks with his own imagination while giving the actor room for personal interpretation.

Miscellaneous Tips

Wherever possible, find the specific **emotions behind** not only the scene, but behind each speech. This is standard work for an actor; you should do it, too. The emotion in a scene usually grows or diminishes according to what's happening. For example, if a character tries to mollify another who's upset, the first's actions could instead further annoy the other. If the point of a scene is an angry explosion, the speeches, as well as the actions, should show the progression from bad to worse. Grounding each speech on its suitable emotional moorings will strengthen the progression of the dialogue within the scene.

Dialogue is best in face-to-face confrontation because confrontation equals conflict. Whenever characters are in conflict, emotion enters the picture. Emotion makes characters say and do things calmer heads would not. Emotion always makes things more interesting because characters act (and say things) more unpredictably.

If you listen to people talk who know each other well, you will learn several things about dialogue and interrelationships. First, when addressing each other, they rarely use the other's name. They already know who they are talking to, so what's the point of calling more attention to it? Who would they be signaling except the audience? If one person wants to emphasize an issue, he might use the other's name, but even this is the exception. If a formal situation occurs where names are used more often, then this can be accommodated in the dialogue to some extent. But each time a character's name is used, the character will most likely sound obsequious. When names are used in every other line of dialogue, it reads and sounds unnatural. When a writer overuses the characters' names in dialogue, it is usually an indication he does not know his creations as well as he should.

When characters are introduced for the first time in a

screenplay, their names do not have to be used right away in dialogue to make sure the viewer gets them. Names can be held until an appropriate moment—perhaps someone will call one's name from across the street, or it will come up naturally in the dialogue. If, within the story, there is a moment when the important characters meet, names can be exchanged. You do not have to be in a rush to label all the characters. In fact, if a few lesser characters are never named, the **economy** of the screenplay will be served. Think of how many people you interact with each day whose names are unknown to you.

When several people are talking in a scene, it can be confusing if you don't use names, especially when one character is speaking directly to another. Still, using a name each time a character talks to someone else sounds false. To make it simpler, use **dialogue cues** to indicate who the character is talking to, like below.

```
                    PHIL
                (to Ed)
          Hey, let's go!
Or:


                    PHIL
                (faces Sally)
          Please, let me go.
```

These cues show the reader and actor what to do. During the film, the viewer sees the speaker turn to Ed or face Sally, and understands who is talking to whom.

The trouble with dialogue cues is that many beginning screenwriters tend to overuse them because they want to direct every line of a speech. If a scene and its dialogue are well written, the emotion will flow with it and the reader will have a good idea whether one character is smiling or frowning. Keep dialogue directions short and only use them if they add something that is not obvious to the speech.

The words "yes" and "no" are used less than one expects in real conversation, people usually nod or shake their heads in response. Whenever a **visual reaction** is possible, use it. This is true for expressing anger as well.

Too often, writers allow their characters to curse indiscriminately. When these words are used in dialogue too frequently, their dramatic value lessens. It is better to find actions which express a character's anger than to call someone names. Then, when someone really wants to swear a blue streak the words will have more power.

Soliloquies and **asides**—techniques used in theater—do not work well in films. In film, people don't talk to themselves and these elements are hard to pull off authentically. Most times in film, they seem forced, unnatural. It's better if the screenwriter finds a different way to get the information across to the audience. The same is true for the nonsequitur. These are hard to follow, whether you read or hear them, so their relevance is often meaningless.

Clichés (e.g., "I've loved you from the very first moment I saw you") find their way into almost everyone's speech now and then, and into almost every writer's first draft. The trouble with these hackneyed phrases in written form is that they stand out, however mundane they are in daily speech. If you want to use them, turn them on their heads. For example, a man might talk about being "strong-armed" by a thug, but another might describe the thug's methods as "a little strong in the arm." Or, "Dead as a thumbtack," not "Dead as a doornail." Or Daffy Duck's, "Just shows to go you!"

Always take time to make the last line of dialogue count. If the final moment is strong, the audience takes it with them when they leave.

Exercises

Take the scene you wrote and reworked at the end of the Chapter Eight. Now, carefully read the dialogue.

> 1. Do all the characters sound the same or does each one have his own voice? This doesn't mean accents, but rather phrasing and word choices that indicate something specific about

them. Think about someone you know who is similar to the character and use him to model the way the character speaks.

2. Do we get a sense of how each character thinks by the way he expresses himself? Is one character cynical while another romantic? Is one humorous? (Humor can be an important tool of the screenwriter and if it can be worked into the dialogue organically, consider doing it.) Again, draw from your own experience of people for models.

3. Is the dialogue clear after reading it the first time? Does it feel real, though still convey the important information? Is it repetitive? (Do too many lines go over the same material?) Does the dialogue duplicate the visual action? Use a red pen or marker to cut the lines which repeat, or which duplicate action.

4. Do the lines in the speeches progress from the least important ideas to the most? Do the lines feel like they're building, or just thrown on the page? Organize the lines so they build to the most intense point in a speech, and ultimately, in the scene.

5. Do any of the lines seem to be "on the nose"? Can these lines be improved by finding actions to convey the points? Have you included any nonverbal language? Look at the places where dialogue is too on-the-nose and try to express the character's attitude or emotions without dialogue. One way to achieve this is for a character to talk about something seemingly unrelated. Does this work better?

6. Do the characters use each other's names too frequently? Do clichés appear in the dialogue? Don't hesitate to delete. But with clichés, try to find more original ways of conveying the expressions.

Now rewrite the scene again. When you finish, read it out loud. Does it sound more focused? Is there a stronger progression? Can you feel the real point of the scene? If not, strengthen the subtext. The next chapter, which discusses subtext in detail, may help.

10

THE SUBTEXT
OF MEANING

The most noticeable results from writing a scene—the overall arrangement of action and dialogue—lead us to, perhaps, the hardest task: delineating the scene's latent meaning. **Scene subtext** is one of the most difficult aspects of screenwriting to grasp. It is what's going on beneath the surface, the undercurrent of emotions and thoughts that truly motivate characters to behave as they do. Most of the time, subtext connects to characters' needs. It can sometimes relate to what characters consciously know and want, yet can't reveal. A story's subtext addresses why characters act and say what they do, before and after plot requirements are considered. Certain actions and dialogue must unfold for the plot to work, but the layer of meaning beneath the plot mechanics goes to the heart of who the characters really are and why they find themselves in a particular story.

Directors and actors bring a scene to life by determining the feelings, thoughts and motives which lie behind the actual words and actions of the characters. If the screenwriter lacks a sufficient understanding of the subtext, his scenes will be lacking in purpose and power. Action will be on the surface, frustrating the directors' and actors' task of realizing the scenes.

Subtext is not what you write, it's what you write around. It is the deeper level of the story which cannot be told so much in words but must be shown in actions. In this chapter, we look at the role of subtext, the emotion beneath the lines, and discuss ways to provide clues to a scene's deeper meaning.

The Role of Subtext

In real life, people rarely say what they feel. More often, they try to hide what bothers them, their personal weaknesses, minor transgressions. They lie about small troubles and big problems. They may be motivated to protect the ones they love or themselves, to gain power or prestige. Because motives are hidden, they often are misperceived. When this happens and problems arise, many of us find ourselves playing the episode over in our minds, trying to figure out exactly what happened and why. The reason? We are fascinated, and usually upset, that our real desires remain so obscure; our words and deeds have miscommunicated our intentions. The real meaning of our actions, the subtext, has been muddled by a pattern of behavior designed to show what we want. But we would prefer people to give us what we need, even if we are not conscious of what that is.

In drama, where art imitates life, our aim is to show a version of reality. The ultimate goal, however, is not to be obscure, but to be understood, to avoid the confusion between needs and wants in everyday life. The screenwriter must know his characters better than they know themselves. The writer demonstrates this knowledge of her characters through the subtext—by letting the audience see what the characters really need beyond what they say they want. The easy way to understand this elusive concept of subtext is to see it as the connection between how the characters, moving according to their desires in a story, end up with what they have needed all along. Cinderella doesn't need a day off work, new slippers or revenge on her family; she needs recognition that comes through love. Lionel, in "Life Lessons," doesn't need romantic or requited love, though he talks nonstop about it; what he needs is sexual frustration, fermented by an unstable personal life, which he channels into creative energy. This need is revealed through subtext. It must be. Lionel himself is not conscious of it.

The screenwriter, therefore, walks a thin line between telling too much and telling too little. Tell too much and you lose the audience's interest. Tell too little and the audience may not understand your story.

Subtext is used to reveal what cannot be easily or honestly told in words. Thus, it has everything to do with needs. A character's need surfaces in the form of feelings and thoughts which generate motives for his actions. In Chapter Two, we defined need as the unconscious motivation of a character. The protagonist has a conscious goal and an unconscious need. If a character's unconscious need contradicts his stated goal, the scene will play differently than if conscious and unconscious minds are in total accord. Need comes from a deep part of the character's psyche of which he may well be ignorant. The character's need may be the real motivation behind everything he does in the story. But for the audience to grasp this fact, the need must be shown in a credible fashion.

Feelings, Thoughts & Motives

To understand a story, certain exposition must be overtly presented to the audience, and other pieces can be implied. Subtext complements exposition by conveying **feelings**, **thoughts** and **motivations** which are too complex to tell in words but which are crucial to understanding a story. At times, the true motives and emotions of a character are the whole point of a film. If this information is clumsily handled or just dumped in the audience's lap, viewers will doubt its veracity, the same way you might be skeptical of a person who tells you his life story at the drop of a hat. A character's motivation carries more weight if it is closely guarded, the way a true motivation is in life. When viewers have to figure out for themselves why characters do something, they become active participants in the dramatic process. When they identify with characters and feel what they are feeling, they are in an active relationship with the material and this participation leads to a deeper involvement in the film.

Through subtext, the screenwriter allows the audience glimpses or hints of the protagonist's and other characters' true feelings and motivations. In "Life Lessons," Lionel tells Paulette he loves her, yet as viewers watch him continually embarrass her, lie to her, try to control and dominate her, they wonder about his definition of love. The subtext is telling us something contrary to what the character says.

The first half of "Hills Like White Elephants" is driven by an unidentified conflict between the couple as they wait for their train. Sure, he's worried about money and she doesn't want to move again, but something much deeper than these concerns fuels the friction between them. When the problem comes out into the open, the audience has seen Davis and Ash both say they will do what the other wants. But by the end of the film, the audience has realized the impossibility of the situation and that what's at stake is nothing less than the couple's relationship.

Subtext & Theme

Subtext should carry a direct relationship to the film's theme, as it becomes the avenue for getting the main ideas across when it would not prove realistic in dialogue. In "Life Lessons," subtext defines the theme. The film isn't about love, but about how the self-absorption of the artist leads to creation. In "Mara Of Rome," the film isn't about the prostitute corrupting the young seminarian; the real topic is the power of faith and love.

When a story is successful, audiences feel satisfied, and that usually means something is working on a deeper level. Even if we can't completely articulate what the story is about, it has touched us in an unaccountable way and it feels true. When we take the time to analyze it, to think about the characters, their feelings and motivations, we make associations that allow the deeper meaning of the film to emerge.

The Emotion Beneath the Lines

Dialogue is the most obvious way to reveal emotion. "I'm really mad," one character says. "I feel sick at heart," says another. Yet, dialogue is rarely the best way to express emotion unless it is forced out into open conversation.

As noted above, when characters tell too much, especially regarding difficult issues, audiences don't assign the matter the proper emotional weight. On the contrary, they tend to trivialize it. Our interest is engaged more deeply seeing a character avoid a troubling issue or when he is unable to find words to express his feelings. We do the same. Our curiosity whetted, we watch more carefully to see what the character will do.

In a scene, the emotion carrying the lines may:

1. Support the dialogue;

2. Contradict the dialogue;

3. Have little relationship to the dialogue.

Emotion-Supporting Dialogue
When emotion supports the dialogue, the lines reflect what the characters feel. For example, happiness is hard to suppress; it affects attitude, actions and easily filters into the conversation. In "Mara Of Rome," when Rosconi arrives at Mara's apartment, he can barely contain his joy; he acts silly and his dialogue is funny. He doesn't need to say he's happy for it is clear from his actions.

171

Fury also is hard to control and it ultimately infiltrates dialogue, too. After Umberto's grandmother reproaches Mara and ruins her peace of mind, Mara can't restrain her anger. She turns it on Rosconi and drives him away. At the beginning of "Life Lessons," Lionel is depressed. He doesn't tell Philip why; he says merely, "I'm going to get slaughtered." When Paulette gets off the jet and sees Lionel waiting for her, she is angry, but she doesn't scream and yell at him; her anger is reflected in her attitude.

Emotional states may be expressed in the dialogue, but still in elliptical ways. Characters talk around the cause of their emotional condition. Even though the dialogue in these scenes is an indirect indication of mood, it must still be properly motivated, usually in a progression of emotions within the scene, or in the progression of scenes that builds emotion.

Emotion Contradicting Dialogue

When emotion contradicts dialogue, the character is forced to take action contrary to his words. He might feel fear yet want to hide it; he might be angry yet behave impassively. Near the beginning of "Life Lessons," Lionel appears in Paulette's room, ostensibly looking for his sable brush, but Paulette sees right through him: "I'm not sleeping with you," she says. He admits an impulse to kiss her foot. She recoils, causing him to let off steam about his upcoming show. Finally, he says, "I just wanted to kiss your foot. I'm sorry. It's nothing personal." Since he has told us how he feels about her, the lines make him sound pitiful because they deny his purported feelings.

In "The Gambler," from *The Gold of Naples*, the boy does not want to play cards with the Count but his father forces him to. Not only must he play, but he must be polite. His sullen boyish look contradicts his formal words, thus expressing his true feelings about the situation.

Emotion with Little Relationship to Dialogue

Sometimes the whole point of a scene is the emotion it contains. The scene is needed to move the audience one way or another. To better identify with or oppose a character approaching a problem. When Paulette calls her mother to ask about coming home, most of the dialogue is incidental. What is that important is the audience witnesses the emotion and pain gripping Paulette, to better understand the depths of her crisis.

In "The Wedding," during the post-nuptial party (where Teresa is introduced to Don Nicola's friends and family) there is a moment when Teresa finds herself alone in the group of strangers. Everyone is curious about her and how she met Don Nicola, since she is from Rome and he is from Naples. The happy guests honor her with a Roman song. One man starts the national anthem but the others find it too stuffy, so they sing a rousing rendition of a drinking tune. We watch as Teresa's doubt and hesitation about her marriage finally give way to happy acceptance. As she joins the singing, we feel her joy. The lyrics of the song, the scene's "dialogue," are meaningless to the real emotion of the scene. This happy moment makes all the more poignant the pain of the revelation at the end.

At the beginning of "Mara Of Rome," the few lines exchanged on the grandmother's patio have little value. What's important is that we see the way the young man looks at the sensual Mara (who is clad only in a luxurious white towel) prancing around her garden. When Mara catches a glimpse at him, we see that her interest is piqued. When she sees his priest's collar, her interest turns to amusement.

Remember, to the audience, your characters are initially strangers. Don't expect viewers to believe everything they say. The audience needs to see them in action and under pressure to discover who they really are.

Revealing The Subtext

Emotions motivate characters to act as they do. The protagonist may be cool and calm, but if all the characters reflect this same indifference, the scenes will not be very interesting. In most scenes, someone is in the grip of an emotion—positive or negative—and this emotion influences the scene, how he behaves and how others interact with him. It also creates interest as we witness people feeling joy or making fools of themselves, or about to embark on a life-threatening quest. Because the audience needs to become aware of the emotions and thoughts affecting the story, the screenwriter must find ways to reveal and to externalize them.

Dialogue

The characteristics of good dialogue have already been discussed in Chapter Nine. Asking a few questions about your characters' emotions can help insure that the dialogue strengthens the subtext. First determine:

1. What must be said in the scene?
2. What can be implied?
3. What doesn't need to be said at all? Then ask:
4. What is the key emotion motivating the characters in this scene?
5. How do their respective emotions specifically affect the characters? What would each do? For example, would one suppress or vent his anger?
6. Would the character have a conscious or unconscious strategy for dealing with this emotion? I.e., would he use understatement or would his words directly contradict his feelings?
7. Is there a progression or a shift in the emotion experienced by a character?
8. Where is the conflict or tension coming from?

Any or all of these questions should help clarify what is going on beneath the surface of the characters. Once these questions have been answered, you should have a better idea of the subtext and how a character might react to it. Dialogue may be the perfect way to bring the subtext into the open, but if it's not, consider the following:

Physical Attitude

Physical attitude refers to a character's outward disposition, or the mood representing his inner emotional state. Body language, facial expressions, and gestures fall under this heading; all provide hints to a character's state of mind. Film is interested in showing what a character is like, as opposed to telling us what he feels, as novels or short stories do. But, screenwriters can't rely on narrative to explain complex personalities, emotions and attitudes. They must figure out ways to clue in the audience through the external action which can be seen and heard.

Lionel's attitude at the beginning of "Life Lessons," shows a man depressed. His whole body sags with the weight of what he is feeling inside: His appearance is a mess, clothes wrinkled, hair unkempt. When Philip mentions the upcoming show, Lionel's face then conveys sheer panic. Contrast this with Lionel's demeanor in the finale (at his exhibition). He stands erect, appearance neat, hair combed, no trace of panic. Above all, Lionel is supremely satisfied with his work.

Rather than narrative, the screenwriter must describe the characteristics of what the audience sees and hears via **action** and **parenthetical directions**. Most of the description is of an external state. In the following portion of a scene, note the action and parenthetical directions and how words are used to describe the characters' attitudes.

```
EXT. TURNER HOUSE—DAY

Indignant eight-year-old ALEC TURNER, dark
eyes flaring, grips the collar of his old
black dog, KING. Across the grass towers 45-
year-old nerd, TED McCLURE. He stands over a
recent brown spot on his immaculate lawn.

                MCCLURE
            (red-faced)
        I am sick and tired of find-
        ing a new pile of crap on my
        way to work every morning!
```

```
                    ALEC
            King didn't do it!

                   MCCLURE
            Look at this!
```

He points with real emotion at the small
circles of dead grass.

Notice how the words "Indignant" and "dark eyes flaring" describe the eight-year-old boy Alec. He "grips" his
dog by the collar as he stands against his neighbor. Does
he grip the dog to hold him back or for protection? The
"nerd" McClure "towers" over brown spots on his lawn.
The **parenthetical cue** lets the reader know McClure's
attitude: He is "red-faced" with anger.

This short introductory description sets the tone for the
rest of the scene. As long as the lines maintain or build on
the established level of intensity, few additional cues are
needed. If, however, the scene reverses (and, say, builds
to an apology), then cues to indicate a turnaround must
be used.

Business

In Chapter Eight we discussed the business of a scene.
Business helps establish a sense of reality. It creates movement which makes film images more visually interesting.
Characters are further defined by what they do within a
scene. The business of doing relates strongly to subtext. If
every action a character takes represents a true portrait of
who she is, her actions speak more truth than the dialogue of ten characters telling us how they feel about her.

The most important business for Lionel in "Life Lessons"
is his painting. Every time he paints, we see his total im-
mersion in the process, his complete commitment to the
work. When he's working, not even his muse Paulette can
call him away.

Lionel's use of the boombox also informs the audience
of his character. As a tool, he uses it in his creative pro-

cess; the music he plays defines his mood and serves as inspiration. But the megawatt stereo also serves as a weapon and illustrates his self-absorption; the music blasts if Lionel is at work, regardless of the hour or who might be trying to sleep. It is a barrier protecting the artist.

Another bit of telling business is Lionel's handling of his basketball. After Lionel has convinced Paulette to stay in New York, he shoots the basketball before he begins painting. One might think he is only warming up, but this action shows he is in a different state. He is no longer depressed and frantic because Paulette is not leaving. Now he can paint, because he can play.

Actions which illustrate emotional states can be very simple. In *Occurrence At Owl Creek*, the protagonist emerges safely from the raging river. Though wounded by Union soldiers, he is free. He stretches his hands and grabs the sand, throwing handfuls of it over his head and into his hair, laughing, overjoyed to be alive. Then he spots one fragile flower growing from the rocks and drags himself over just to smell it. All of this underscores his joy at escaping the hangman's noose. The simplicity of these actions as expressions make them seem all the more real and poignant.

Atmosphere

Atmosphere helps reveal the characters' inner states by reinforcing them. Nature, time of day or year, contribute to creating a mood which reflects the interior world of the characters. Using the external world to mirror the inner emotions felt by the characters helps the audience share in the characters' experiences.

In "Life Lessons," much of Lionel's painting takes place at night, when others sleep and dream. The nocturnal mood reinforces that artists are in touch with a dreamlike creativity most everyday mortals miss.

Atmosphere reflects Paulette's emotional state in "Life Lessons," too. After the performance artist rejects her overtures, she furiously leaves the club. Lionel follows her into the rain, offering to kill the guy if that's what she wants. Crying, she vents her frustration and embarrassment by blaming Lionel for Stark's insensitivity. The pouring rain heightens the desolate feeling both have because of the impossible situation between them.

A few moments later, Lionel finds Paulette at home. The tone of the film turns considerably darker as he threatens her. "I could do anything to you," he tells her, including rape or murder. "Because I'm nothing to you, I'm the invisible man." Playing the scene at night, in the shadowy kitchen accentuates the ominous note in his voice. She is not safe here at the hearth; it's dark, she's alone, facing the naked rage of a man she's depersonalized.

Exercises

Probably one of the most important books a committed screenwriter can read is Constantin Stanislavski's *An Actor Prepares*. Not only does it give important insights into how actors work, but these same methods can be used by a writer to discover the emotions motivating characters, thus providing a key to the subtext in a scene.

A good exercise for revealing subtext is to take a character in a situation akin to the protagonist in *Occurrence At Owl Creek*. When he reaches shore, how does he express his joy? He throws sand in the air and on himself as he laughs. He sees a flower and goes to smell it.

1. Create a situation where a character will experience strong emotions, e.g., joy or rage, sadness or satisfaction.

2. Characterize the feeling you choose.

3. What does the character do or say? How does he express these feelings?

4. Use a minimum of dialogue to express the character's inner state. Think of visual images and sound effects which will help the audience

identify the feelings in the scene. Think of incidents and the atmosphere and how they can support the emotion.

5. Try this exercise with different characters and different emotions. The exercises will expand the craft of your writing.

PART FOUR

Keeping
Focused

11

KEEPING FOCUSED: WHAT DOES MY PROTAGONIST REALLY WANT?

One of the toughest obstacles a screenwriter faces, whether beginner or veteran, writing a feature or short, is keeping the story focused. However, where a feature might survive an inventive interlude away from its main theme, a short film screenplay that strays from its central topic for more than a moment, can mean failure.

There are many indications a screenplay has lost its focus. Contradictory feedback from an early draft is usually the result of an unfocused screenplay. The writer has too many ideas competing for attention, causing him to lose grip of his characters, plot and theme; resulting in a plotless story, a loss of momentum or just a general lack of understanding. **Writer's block** is another symptom of a screenplay whose purpose has become ill-defined. The imagination dries up and words won't come, often leaving the writer frustrated and depressed.

In this, the final chapter, we look at a few strategies for keeping a film on track and writer's block at bay.

Keeping on Track

When a screenplay begins to wander because of too many ideas competing for attention, or if writer's block strikes, the best way to get back on track is to return to the two questions asked in Chapter One:

1. What is the story about?
2. What does the protagonist really want?

What Is The Story About?

Coming back to the first question can remind a writer what she originally found interesting and exciting in the material. It's inevitable that as a work-in-progress develops, it will change. A theme or controlling idea that led you to write the story may bear little resemblance to the central idea found in the finished draft. The theme may have changed without you being aware of it.

To discover what the story is really about, you have to look at the screenplay as a whole and determine what the **unifying idea** is. If one isn't self-evident, guess at what the screenplay suggests as its theme. Simply state it, then ask whether the material has been motivated in some way by this **central idea**. If you can't state your theme and you don't know what the film is really about anymore, try these few ideas to uncover it.

The fundamental qualities which lead to a protagonist's success or failure hold the answers to what you are writing about. First, look at the hero. If he succeeds at his goal, what special quality enabled him to succeed? If he failed to achieve his goal, what led to this failure, and what did the antagonist have that made it possible for him to win? The answers to these questions should help you learn what your film is about. However, in order to help you, the answers must be clear. You can ask yourself later if a theme is valid or adequately motivated, but first you have to know what it is.

What Does My Protagonist Really Want?

This question holds the real key to success in getting a screenplay back on track, and it is the most important question to ask. Many screenplays wander because writers forget what their protagonists want or need. Sometimes the protagonist's want and need are undeveloped or underemphasized, causing their relevance on the screenplay to be lost and the plot to break down. In other cases, the protagonist's want or need may not be compelling enough to involve the audience, or they may not be believable.

A protagonist must have a clear goal and/or need which drives the character and screenplay forward. Every scene must depend in some way on the **driving action**, of revealing character and information which motivate and stoke the central conflict as it rises to the crisis and climax. The driving force demands that other characters react and oppose your hero. These interactions should lead to a direct cause-and-effect relationship from one scene to another which, in turn, keeps the plot linked. If the scenes of the plot are interdependent, that is, if one scene leads inexorably to the next, thematic problems can be more easily discerned.

The character's want or need must be introduced by the setup of a screenplay. It can be in place before the story opens, as in "Life Lessons," or grow out of the opening situation, as in "The Man In The Brooks Brothers Shirt." Many short screenplays stall right at the beginning because the protagonist's story goal doesn't emerge soon enough. Short films are just that—short. You must create tension in quick order to hook the audience. Establishing your goal as early as possible helps capture your audience by getting them to ask: Will your hero get what he wants (and/or needs)?

185

If the character's want or need is not compelling enough for the audience to identify with, the screenplay will not be affecting. The protagonist's want/need must be definite and forceful to win sympathy and hold the audience's attention. If it isn't, then it must be rethought. The problem of creating a compelling want/need may sometimes be solved by including scenes which show the emotional consequences of the action the protagonist has inspired. An example from "Life Lessons" shows that Lionel feels guilty after fighting with Paulette. Playing these scenes gives a human dimension to the characters and conflict. Humanizing characters makes it easier for the audience to identify with them.

If a protagonist's want or need is not believable, it must be replaced by one that is.

The Antagonist

A primary antagonist gives strength and clarity to a screenplay. As locus of the opposing force, he makes the conflict distinct and understandable. Just like the protagonist, the antagonist must have a want and need. The same questions above apply to him. What does he really want and need? Is it sufficient to drive the story to conflict with the protagonist? If not, how can you make it so that it will be?

A short film can survive having no main antagonist to oppose your protagonist. If so, the controlling idea or theme must be all the stronger and clearer to bind the drama together and gain the audience's attention.

These questions can serve as the basis for evaluating the comments you receive about your work. More importantly, the answers to these questions can help guide you back to the source of all satisfying drama—your characters—by insuring they have conflicting wants and needs that drive the story forward.

Conclusion

Writing a good screenplay, short or long, is a difficult job. There are no magic formulas which insure success other than those timeless elements of a strong premise, compelling characters, a powerful story and a valid theme. Approach your material in a fresh and inventive way and do not be afraid to rewrite, rewrite and rewrite some more.

The best short films embrace complex, personal issues; feature films tend to stay away from these kinds of themes. Often complex, personal issues are the source of the short film's success. Their plots do not have to be complicated, but their characters do. The characters' wants and needs should be strong, specific, and clear enough to drive the story. Try giving your protagonist a central problem to cope with, as well as related subproblems, then let the plot flow from these dilemmas.

Think of the plot as the story you tell to explain how a character changes from his initial state to his new state in the end. The focus on character pushing plot, and not the other way around, is what distinguishes all good drama and literature. While other dramatic arenas may have lost their focus on character as the defining story element in short films, characters thrive. They are why the art form exists—to explore the obvious and inner nuances of what a character thinks he wants, and really needs—and then to make visual the reconciliation between these wants and needs. Your short film will then be as complex, intriguing, exciting and, ultimately, as satisfying as your lead character.

In this book, I've attempted to outline the basic requirements of a successful short film, contrasting them with those of a feature-length film, while showing that both are based on the same fundamental principles. If you can write an effective short film, chances are you can write a good feature-length screenplay, too. Good luck!

Appendix A

Fade In To Fade Out:
Proper Screenplay Format

A screenplay is a blueprint for a film. Screenplay form reflects this, having evolved over the years into a particular arrangement of styles which easily communicates the necessary information needed to make a film. Production managers, set designers, actors, etc., all must have easy access to the information they need to do their job. Proper form indicates a film's approximate length and budget. It allows production managers to break down the screenplay, indicates to art directors what kinds of sets are needed, and easily identifies each actor's lines.

Most screenplays are written in **master scenes**, which present the action in the clearest form—<u>without</u> camera angles and with only a few stage directions. It communicates simply what happens in the scene, letting the action be the focus and not the camera.

Scene headings, **action**, **characters' names**, **parenthetical directions** and **dialogue** are the essential elements every screenwriter must use, but there are other format characteristics screenwriters must know as well. For example, introducing new characters, writing such **transitions** as "DISSOLVE TO" and even "FADE OUT" require as much adherence to format as scene headings and action. Hour-long and long-form teleplays (screenplays for television) are written in a similar format, though there are superficial differences. Situation comedies, on the other hand, have a formatting configuration all their own.

In this appendix, we present the fundamental aspects and jargon of screenplay formatting.

Fade In: Scene Headings

A screenplay usually begins with FADE IN:. These words are always typed on the left-hand margin. Double-spaced below FADE IN is the **scene heading** designating the location of the first scene. The scene heading is always in capitals and always gives the same basic information in the same order. This information is:

    1. INT. or EXT.
    2. LOCATION
    3. TIME—DAY or NIGHT

It should look like this:

`EXT. TURNER HOUSE—DAY`

The scene heading almost always begins with INT. or EXT., indicating either the scene takes place inside or outside. The abbreviated form is always used. INT. or EXT. is followed by the exact location in which the scene takes place, and then the time of day. Every time the location changes, the scene heading must change, indicating a new scene.

Time is denoted by DAY or NIGHT, though occasionally SUNRISE or SUNSET, DAWN or DUSK are used. An exact time in the heading is not necessary; day or night tells the reader all she needs to know. Once time has been established, it does not have to be repeated in each new scene heading until the time changes. Often, screenwriters will pick up the time again, whether it has shifted from night to day or day to night, once the location of the scene changes. Note that a dash separates the "where" from the "when" of the scene.

The scene heading is brief and specific. It allows the reader to orient himself quickly to the scene. It also makes essential information easily accessible for the actual production of the screenplay.

There are exceptions to every rule. Suppose a writer doesn't want to fade in on the scene, but wants to use sound to create a mood before actually beginning the visual part of the film. The writer might try something like this:

```
A BLACK SCREEN

The SOUND of drums pounds in the distance.

FADE IN:

EXT. CONGO RIVER—NIGHT

The mile-wide waterway splits the jungle.
```

Here, the words "FADE IN" are not really necessary and could be dropped.

There are also exceptions to the use of INT. or EXT. When an overall location serves for a series of actions remaining inside or outside, this abbreviation can be dropped from the scene heading. Note below:

```
INT. BARN—DAY

A boy runs for the ladder.

IN THE LOFT

Five kittens nuzzle next to their mother. The
boy climbs into the loft and joins the cats.
```

Or:

```
EXT. CONGO RIVER—NIGHT

The sky blazes burnt-orange as smoke billows
over the trees. A small boat motors up the
river.

AROUND A BEND

The boat continues toward a village afire in
the night.
```

For the examples above, each second scene could easily begin with INT. or EXT. and be considered correct form. These formatting rules are not absolutes, rules which al-

ways have to be followed; The screenwriter has some lee-
way to describe his vision in a screenplay.

The location of the scene must be specific, but it should
not be cluttered. If the scene takes place on a busy street,
all that is needed in the scene heading is "STREET." That
the street is in a busy city can be put in the description
following the heading.

Another element sometimes used in a scene heading is
"POV," which stands for "point of view." It is used to indicate what a character is seeing.

```
JOHN'S POV—THE SILVER JAGUAR
```

The car lies inelegantly on its side, wrapped
around a tree.

Or:

```
INT./EXT. BUS—JOHN'S POV
```

The silver Jaguar lies on its side, wrapped
around a tree.

Both descriptions tell us what the camera sees, but one
also tells where the shot originates. The one thing to remember when using POV in a scene heading is to indicate
when the shot returns to the master scene. It can be confusing to the reader if the action shifts from a character's
point of view back to the master scene without indication.

A **master scene** is a specific configuration of action,
information, and dialogue, consisting of a scene heading,
a narrative description of the scene action, speaking characters' names, dialogue and parenthetical directions. It
looks like this:

```
EXT. TURNER HOUSE—DAY
```

Indignant eight-year-old ALEC TURNER, dark
eyes flaring, grips the collar of his old
black dog, KING. Across the grass towers 45-
year-old nerd, TED McCLURE. He stands over a
recent brown spot on his immaculate lawn.

```
              MCCLURE
           (red-faced)
    I am sick and tired of find-
    ing a new pile of crap on my
    way to work every morning!

              ALEC
    King didn't do it!

              MCCLURE
    Look at this!

He points with real emotion at the small
circles of dead grass.
```

A master scene sets the location and time, then lets the action unfold without cluttering up the scene with camera moves and angles. It allows the characters' story to develop without the reader having to take time to put himself in place of the camera for every shot. A good screenwriter working in master scenes presents the action in such a way that the reader sees the screenplay unfold as he does when writing it.

Along with POV, there are a few other descriptions which find their way into a scene heading. AERIAL VIEW indicates we are seeing something from high above.

```
AERIAL VIEW—TOKYO—DAY

The city sprawls amorphously below rain
clouds. Its clogged expressways spiral out
from the center: The Emperor's Palace.
```

Insert is used to draw the reader's and audience's attention to something specific, as in the contents of a letter, a special insignia, a detail of jewelry, or anything not immediately distinguishable in the master scene.

```
INSERT—LETTER
              In smudgy type:
    Dear John,
    I hope you have found the emerald
    ring and are on your way back home.
```

An insert shows close-up the specific information needed to follow the story. It tells the reader how this information will be handled on the screen for the audience.

POVs, AERIAL VIEW, INSERT should all be employed sparingly. These techniques should be used when information essential to the plot can't be given any other way, or when the writer is going for a specific effect.

The Action

After the scene heading comes the description of the **action**. Use a double-space between the scene heading and the description of action. The actual description is single-spaced. If there is more than one paragraph of action, double-space between them. The description paragraphs use normal left and right margins.

```
EXT. TURNER HOUSE—DAY

Indignant eight year-old ALEC TURNER, dark
eyes flaring, grips the collar of his old
black dog, KING.
```

The action is always written in the present tense; it should be clear and to the point; otherwise, information necessary for that scene will be obscured. It's best to be lucid yet vivid, creating scenes that come alive on the page.

When **characters** appear in a screenplay for the first time, their names are CAPITALIZED. For the important characters, a brief description should follow; supplying only enough information to give a mental snapshot, not a complete biography. What characters do and say provide truer clues to their real natures. After the characters' initial introductions, their names are no longer capitalized in the action (although whenever they have dialogue, names should be capitalized on the character names' margin).

Important **sound directions** in the action also appear in capital letters. The door SLAMS. The tire POPS. The gun FIRES. These caps flag specific sound cues for the soundtrack.

Sometimes, to call attention to them, important props are capitalized. For instance, a piece of scenery might play a significant role in the screenplay; by capitalizing it, the reader is less likely to skim over it.

Characters Names' Margin

The characters names' margin is typed approximately in the center of the page, but it is not center-justified. It is two and a half to three inches from the left hand margin. The length of a character's name makes no difference; whether it is Bob or Bronowski, the names always begin at the same setting. A center-justified name margin is a sure sign of an amateur screenplay.

In this margin, the characters' names are always CAPITALIZED. The description of the action is always two spaces above the character's name. Occasionally, a name will be followed by one of several parenthetical cues. These can be (V.O.) for voice-over, (O.S.) or (O.C.) for off-screen or camera, or (CONT'D) for a speech that has been broken up by a page break and continues to the next page. These parenthetical cues are not the same as parenthetical directions which are character directions.

When dialogue is broken up by a page break, (MORE) should appear on the last line before the break starting at the characters name's margin. For example:

```
                ALEC
       Mom, could I get a raise in
       my allowance?

                SUSAN
       A raise? How come?

                ALEC
       I deserve one. Since I have

            (MORE)
```

The page break cuts the speech. At the top of the next page, the character's name should appear followed by (CONT'D) and the rest of the speech, like this:

```
              ALEC (CONT'D)
    to clean up Mr. McClure's
    lawn, too.
```

Parenthetical Directions & Dialogue

Parenthetical directions are instructions for character reactions. Parentheticals can also be brief stage directions describing what the character is doing while speaking. They can be included right after the character's name or in the middle of dialogue to emphasize emotion or direct action. Parentheticals never come at the end of a speech. If action needs to be staged or emotion emphasized when a character finishes speaking, these directions should be included as action.

Note in the scene above that the last line, which is a stage direction for McClure, returns to the action margin. It is not written like this:

```
              MCCLURE
    Look at this!
              (points with real
              emotion at the
              small circles of
              dead grass)
```

Including this much description within parenthetical directions tends to clutter the page, and creates a clumsy look. Parenthetical margins run about two inches from the left-hand margin and about two or two and a half inches from the right. The style of the parentheticals is unusual. If there is more than one line of direction, the second line indents one character. It looks like this:

```
              ALEC
       (spins and hugs his
        mother)
    I don't want to go!
```

The lines the characters speak are **dialogue**. These margins begin approximately one inch to one and a half inches from the left-hand margin and one and a half inches from the right-hand margin. The left-hand margin is always justified, while the right margin is not. It is important not to let the dialogue spill too far past its right-hand margin; if it does, it can be confused with the action.

It is always single-spaced between the character's name, the parenthetical directions and the dialogue. Double spaces are used between character speeches.

Transitions

Transitions indicate movement from one scene to the next. They can be instantaneous or gradual. All transitions (except for the first FADE IN:) start approximately five inches from the left-hand margin and are double-spaced below the described action. Generally, CUT TO: is not used after every scene since a cut is the normal way to move from scene to scene.

Sometimes, though, screenwriters will use "SHOCK CUT TO:" or "SMASH CUT TO:" for dramatic purposes. This kind of punctuation is used to make a point or to dramatically separate scenes or scene sequences.

"DISSOLVE TO:" means one image fades away as another fades in to replace it, and it usually indicates that time has passed. However, it is used less and less frequently in the industry.

The last transition used in a screenplay is FADE OUT: it does not have to be followed by a colon, though sometimes it is. Most often, a period comes after it, denoting the end. Many screenwriters opt to follow "fade out" with THE END. When used, "the end" goes in the characters names' margin:

THE END

A Note on Screenwriting Software

There are many computer screenwriting software programs currently on the market. They can either format your script as you type it, or format a document into screenplay form before it prints. Of course, it's also possible to construct a style sheet with macros and quick keys, enabling you to type from screenplay format in any word processing program. But the question is, do you want to spend your time writing a screenplay or writing a program? When screenplays are not properly formatted, everyone's job in the production of a film becomes harder. And when you graduate to writing feature-length screenplays, script formatting becomes one of the easiest ways to distinguish a pro from an amateur.

Screenwriting programs are more than worth the cost, especially those which format as you type and allow changes to a script, either with automatic accommodation to the current draft or via the creation of separate drafts. Stand-alone programs such as Final Draft (Mac/Windows), Movie Master (Windows/DOS), ScriptThing (Windows/DOS) and Scriptware (DOS/Windows) allow you to write in the correct format as soon as you start up. Cross-platform programs such as ScriptWizard (Windows) and ScriptTools (Mac/Windows) are designed to use macro features found in specific word processing programs like Microsoft Word or WordPerfect. Scriptor (Mac/DOS), the grandfather of screenplay formatting programs, is not the program to use during the creation of your screenplay, but once it is written and in a recognizable format, it will format it by adding page numbers, automatically break speeches automatically with (MORE) and (CONT'D) exactly where they belong, and add (CONTINUED) at the top and bottom of the required pages.

The time you spend formatting your screenplay program can be better spent working on your story, or rewriting it. Because computer complications often are used by those looking for excuses not to write, use a program (following the above format guidelines) to format a script and your brain to focus on the story.

Locating Screenplay Software Programs

Most screenwriting programs can be found where computer programs are sold. Some companies will send you a free demo disk. Below is a list of the main screenwriting programs used in Hollywood, their telephone numbers and internet or E-Mail addresses if you are looking for information.

Software & E-Mail Address	Phone Numbers
Final Draft www.bcsoftware.com/bchome	800-231-4055
Movie Master mmsupport@aol.com	201-251-1979
Scriptor scriptor@screenplay.com	800-84-STORY
ScriptThing kenschafer@aol.com or compuserve.com/homepages/scriptthing	800-450-9450
ScriptTools 72154.1251@compuserve.	800-464-7511
Scriptware http://scriptware.com	800-788-7090
ScriptWizard swarren@aol.com or 71531.1300@compuserve.com	818-500-7081
SideBySide SimonSkil@aol.com or simon1@concentric.com	888-234-6789

Appendix B

Referenced Films Available on Video

"Life Lessons" from *New York Stories*
(TOUCHSTONE PICTURES) 1989
Writer: Richard Price
Director: Martin Scorsese
Video Distributor: TOUCHSTONE HOME VIDEO
  c/o Walt Disney Home Video
  500 South Buena Vista Street
  Burbank, CA 91521-7145

"Mara Of Rome" from *Yesterday, Today And Tomorrow**
(Carlo Ponti Productions) 1964
Writer: Cesare Zavattini
Director: Vittorio De Sica
Video Distributor: JEF FILMS, Film House
  143 Hickory Hill Circle
  Osterville, MA 02655
  (508) 428-7198

"Anna Of Milan" from *Yesterday, Today And Tomorrow*
(Carlo Ponti Productions) 1964
Writers: Cesare Zavattini & Billa Billa,
Short Story by Alberto Moravia
Director: Vittorio De Sica
Video Distributor: JEF FILMS, Film House, see above

Peel from Films by Jane Campion
Writer/Director: Jane Campion
Video Distributor: FIRST RUN FEATURES
  153 Waverly Place
  New York, NY 10014
  (212) 243-0600

201

"The Man In The Brooks Brothers Shirt"
from *Women & Men: Stories Of Seduction*
(HBO SHOWCASE) 1990
Writer/Director: Frederic Raphael, adapted from Mary
　　　　McCarthy's short story, The Man in the Brooks
　　　　Brothers Shirt
Video Distributor: FACETS MULTIMEDIA
　　　　1517 West Fullerton Avenue
　　　　Chicago, IL 60614
　　　　(800) 5-FACETS

"Hills Like White Elephants"
from *Women & Men: Stories Of Seduction*
(HBO SHOWCASE) 1990
Writers: Joan Didion & John Gregory Dunne
Director: Tony Richardson
Video Distributor: FACETS MULTIMEDIA, see above

Occurrence At Owl Creek (1962)
Writer/Director: Robert Enrico
Video Distributor: VIDEO YESTERYEAR
　　　　Box C
　　　　Sandy Hook, CT 06482
　　　　(203) 744-2476

The Red Balloon* (1955)
Writer/Director: Albert Lamorisse
Video Distributor: NEW LINE HOME VIDEO
　　　　116 North Robertson Blvd.
　　　　Los Angeles, CA 90048
　　　　(310) 854-5811

"The Dutch Master," from *Tales Of Erotica*****
(TRIMARK) 1995
Writers: Susan Seidelman and Jonathan Brett
Director: Susan Seidelman
Video Distributor: VIDMARK ENTERTAINMENT
        A Division of TRIMARK
        2644 30th Street
        Santa Monica, CA 90405-3009
        (310) 314-2000

Ray's Male Heterosexual Dance Hall** (1987)
Writer/Director: Bryan Gordon
Video Distributor: JCI Video
        At the time of printing, this distributor
        is out of business

"The Wedding" from *The Gold Of Naples* (1954)
Writer: Cesare Zavattini
Director: Vittorio De Sica
Video Distributor: VIDEO YESTERYEAR
        Box C
        Sandy Hook, CT 06482
        (203) 744-2476

"The Gambler" from *The Gold Of Naples* (1954)
Writer: Cesare Zavattini Director: Vittorio De Sica
Distributor: VIDEO YESTERYEAR, see above

The Thoroughbred
Writer: Kent Danne
Director: Harold Huth
Video Distributor: RHINO HOME VIDEO
        2225 Colorado Avenue
        Santa Monica, CA 90404

Twist Of Fate (1993)
Writer-Director: Douglas Kunin
Video Distributor: THRESHOLD FILMS
        5919 Tuxedo Terrace
        Los Angeles, CA 90068
        (213) 464-4057

FACETS MULTIMEDIA, in Chicago, will rent by mail from their catalogue. A membership costs $25 a year, for which you receive two rental tapes. Additional rentals are $10 per tape. A credit card is needed. FACETS also has a Critics Membership at $100 a year, which includes twelve rentals. Additional rentals are $10 per tape. A free sample catalogue can be obtained by writing to them:

        FACETS MULTIMEDIA
        Rentals Department
        1517 West Fullerton Ave.
        Chicago, IL 60614
        (800) 5-FACETS

A full catalogue is $7.95 plus shipping and handling.

    *   Academy Award winner, Best Foreign Film
   **   Academy Award winner,
        Best Live Action Short Film
  ***   Academy Award winner, Best Screenplay
 ****   Nominated for an Academy Award, in the Live
        Action Short category

Appendix C

General Film Index

TITLES WITH AUTHORS OR ADAPTORS OF SCREENPLAY

Ace Ventura: Pet Detective, Tom Shadyac, Jack Bernstein, Jim Carrey

The Appointments of Dennis Jennings, Mike Armstrong & Steven Wright

Black Rider, Pepe Danquart

Blazing Saddles, Mel Brooks, Norman Steinberg, Andrew Bergman, Richard Pryor, Alan Unger

Chicks in White Satin, Elaine Holliman

Chinatown, Robert Towne

The Crying Game, Neil Jordan

Dances with Wolves, Michael Blake

Especially on Sunday
   "The Blue Dog," Tonino Guerra

Franz Kafka's It's a Wonderful Life, Peter Capaldi

Ghost, Bruce Joel Rubin

Glengarry Glen Ross, David Mamet

Glory, Kevin Jarre

The Gold of Naples
   "The Gambler," Cesare Zavattini
   "The Wedding," Cesare Zavattini

Groundhog Day, Daniel F. Rubin, Harold Ramis

"Hills Like White Elephants," Joan Didion, John Gregory Dunne

Jerry Maguire, Cameron Crowe

Jurassic Park, David Koepp, Michael Crichton

The Last Temptation of Christ, Paul Schrader

Lawrence of Arabia, Robert Bolt

Lethal Weapon, Shane Black

The Lunch Date, Adam Davidson

The Macomber Affair, Casey Robinson, Seymour Bennett

"The Man In The Brooks Brothers Shirt," Frederic Raphael
Mrs. Doubtfire, Randi Mayem Singer, Leslie Dixon
Never Cry Wolf, Curtis Hanson, Sam Hamm
New York Stories
    "Life Lessons," Richard Price
Norma Rae, Harriet Frank, Jr., Irving Ravetch
The Nutty Professor, David Sheffield, Barry W. Blaustein,
    Tom Shadyac, Steve Oedekerk
Occurrence at Owl Creek, Robert Enrico
The Old Man and the Sea, Peter Viertel
Omnibus, Sam Karmann
Peel, Jane Campion
The Piano, Jane Campion
Platoon, Oliver Stone
Pretty Woman, J. F. Lawton
Quiz Show, Paul Attanasio
Raising Arizona, Ethan Coen, Joel Coen
Ray's Male Heterosexual Dance Hall, Bryan Gordon
Sense And Sensibility, Emma Thompson
Shine, Jan Sardi, Story by Scott Hicks
The Red Balloon, Albert Lamorisse
Tales of Erotica
    "The Dutch Master," Susan Seidelman, Jonthan Brett
Tootsie, Larry Gelbart, Murray Schisgal, Don McGuire
Trading Places, Herschel Weingrod, Timothy Harris
Unforgiven, David Peoples
War of the Roses, Michael Leeson
Witness, William Kelly, Earl W. Wallace, Pamela Wallace
Yesterday, Today and Tomorrow
    "Anna of Milan," Cesare Zavattini
    "Mara of Rome," Cesare Zavattini, Billa Billa

APPENDIX D

The Writer's Reference Shelf

Here are a few books, besides those listed in the bibliography, that can prove helpful. A few are geared to feature films, but all are valuable additions to a writer's reference shelf. Most are available in paperback or in libraries.

The Elements Of Style by Wm. Strunk, Jr. and E.B. White; MacMillan. Read this before you write another word.

The Art Of Dramatic Writing by Lajos Egri, 1960; Simon & Schuster. Much of what Egri has to say about the dramatic form is applicable to short stories, novels, plays and screenplays, short or long. The chapter on Premise is especially important. The writing style is archaic, but if you can understand what he's talking about and apply it to your work, then this book will prove invaluable.

The Tools Of Screenwriting: A Writer's Guide To The Craft And Elements Of A Screenplay by David Howard & Edward Mably, 1993; St. Martin's Press. A good book on the basic concepts of the craft of screenwriting. Very valuable from start to finish, to the short-form filmmaker or to the long.

Writing Great Characters: The Psychology Of Character Development In Screenplays by Michael Halperin, Ph.D., 1996; Lone Eagle Publishing Co. A wonderful examination of character from a screenwriter's viewpoint. And:

Characters & Viewpoint by Scott Card, 1988; Writer's Digest Books. A good book on how to build characters and use the proper voice for your story.

How To Write & Sell Your Sense Of Humor by Gene Perret, 1982; Writer's Digest Books. A good primer on humor, jokes and comedy.

Making A Good Script Great by Linda Seger, 1994; Dodd, Mead & Co. Primarily about rewriting a feature screenplay, but she has great ideas and puts dramatic concepts in easily understandable language.

The Writer's Journey, by Christopher Vogler, 1992; Michael Wiese Productions. For anyone prepared to go the distance. Also:

The Hero With A Thousand Faces by Joseph Campbell, 1972; Princeton University Press. A guide for living as well as writing.

The Art And Craft Of Novel Writing by Oakley Hall; Writer's Digest Books. As the title indicates, this is primarily for novelists, but there is helpful information that can be applied to writing in general.

The Writer's Survival Guide: How To Cope With Rejection, Success, And 99 Other Hang-Ups Of The Writing Life by Jean Rosenbaum and Veryl Rosenbaum, 1982; Writer's Digest Books. For later on, when the process of writing starts to get to you.

I Can See You Naked: A Fearless Guide To Making Great Presentations by Ron Hoff, 1988; Andrews & McMeel. An excellent book if you have to pitch a story idea.

How To Sell Yourself by Joe Girard, 1979; Warner Books. Written by a car salesman, but there is a lot of useful information on motivation, attitude, self-confidence and communication that can be applied to selling yourself to people in the film and publishing business.

How To Sell Anything To Anybody by Joe Girard, 1977; Warner Books. *See above.*

The Business Of Being A Writer by Stephen Goldin and Kathleen Sky, 1982; Harper and Row. Very good for the business side of writing: contracts, dealing with editors, submissions, etc.

No list would be complete without:

Adventures In The Screen Trade by William Goldman, 1983; Warner Books. A fascinating look at the creative and critical process with great insights into the film industry.

APPENDIX E

RAY'S MALE HETEROSEXUAL
DANCE HALL

WRITTEN BY

BRYAN GORDON

FADE IN:

BIG BAND MUSIC

CAMERA MOVES DOWN A TALL OFFICE
BUILDING...

We hear the voice of Sam Logan, early thirties...

>   SAM (V.O.)
>   I used to feel I was a part
>   of those office buildings.
>   After all, I once had an
>   office there. Okay, I didn't
>   have an office with a view.
>   But I was headed for a view.
>   A good view...

and the camera settles on a nearby park—noon

SMALL CHILDREN play. OLD PEOPLE sit. BLUE and
WHITE COLLAR WORKERS, walk in a brisk and
leisurely clip. OTHER WORKERS sit on benches,
the ground and blankets eating their lunches.

THE CAMERA FINDS:

SAM LOGAN on a bench—mid-thirties, a suit and
tie, feeds some peanuts to some PIGEONS. He
casually watches an ATTRACTIVE WOMAN pass.

>   SAM (V.O.)
>   That of course was all be-
>   fore FabTek, the company I
>   worked for became WellPeck
>   and left me out of a job.
>   There I go again, dwelling.
>   I just can't keep blaming
>   myself for all of this.
>   Fabtek merged with WellPeck.
>   It happens everyday. Ah-
>   Anyway, I was killing some
>   time and preparing for my
>   next job interview, United
>   Cracktel, going over in my
>   head why I wanted to work
>   for a place like United
>   Cracktel when I ran into
>   Cal...

CAL, a clean-cut upbeat businessman in his mid-thirties, walks briskly by. He recognizes Sam and walks over to him.

> SAM (V.O.)
> ... a friend of mine I worked with years ago. The guy had success written all over his face...

Sam and Cal warmly shake each other's hands in a business-like manner and Cal sits down. Sam is a bit self-conscious. They begin talking.

> SAM (V.O.)
> I instantly plunged into my own saga of job interview, telling him that everyone tells me I look great on paper, decent resume the whole bit. Just seems like I don't make the right con-tacts...

> CAL
> (Self-assured)
> Contacts, Sam, that's the attitude.

> SAM
> Yeah, contacts, I know, but where, how?

> SAM (V.O.)
> He looked at me as if I never participated in soci-ety.

> CAL
> I know it's tough being out of work, Sam.

> SAM
> Oh, very tough. Very Tough. If I seem overly anxious, it's...I am—

> CAL
> You do. It's the old cliche, it's who you know...

213

                    SAM
Why didn't I ever believe
that?...

                    CAL
People simply kill each
other...

                    SAM
I always thought the
cream...

                    CAL
Would rise to the top.

                    SAM (V.O.)
He finished my cliche. Let
me finish my cliche.

                    CAL
        (Looks at watch)
Listen, I'd love to talk to
you, but I'm on my way to
find a new position.

                    SAM
        (Surprised)
I thought you had a great
position.

                    CAL
        (Confident)
Oh, I do. But you're never
secure. I'm always looking.
You've got to constantly
know and meet the right
people.

                    SAM (V.O.)
The right people. There must
be a constant turnover of
the right people.

                    SAM
So, it's the contacts.

                    CAL
Contacts.

                    SAM (V.O.)
Contacts.

                        CAL
You're not going to find a
job, the right job, at an
ordinary job interview. I'm
sorry.

                   SAM (V.O.)
He's right.

                        SAM
                   (Pressing)
So where do you make the
right contacts?

                        CAL
                   (Milking)
Where? Lot of people ask me
where.

                        SAM
                   (impatient)
Yeah, Well, so, where?

                        CAL
There's only one place to
meet the right people, Sam.

                        SAM
                   (Blurting)
I-I—Where!

                        CAL
                   (Beat)
Sam, why don't you come with
me. Forget your job interview. There's only one
place.
                   (Direct)
Ray's Male Heterosexual
Dance Hall.

                                    CUT TO:

WE HEAR ANOTHER UP TEMPO—BIG BAND SOUND.

OUTDOOR SIGN: "RAY'S MALE HETEROSEXUAL DANCE
HALL"

INT. RAY'S MALE HETEROSEXUAL DANCE HALL—NOON

ANOTHER SIGN: STOCK EXCHANGE QUOTES

The camera tilts down to a crowded bar, filled
with executives in suits.

Cal leads Sam through a packed, narrow bar
area filled with HETEROSEXUAL MEN all dressed
in suits and ties. A bartender's BARTENDER
pours drinks. Trophies and TV set adorn the
bar. The atmosphere is mixed with smoke,
drinking, nibbling, talk, winking, hand
shakes, darting eyes, back slapping, laughter,
and distant ballroom music.

> SAM (V.O.)
> This is where everybody is.
> No wonder no one's around
> lunchtime. They're all here.

ANGLE

Sam and Cal spring out of the packed narrow
bar area.

> SAM (V.O.)
> Wow, what a place. Hey. I
> know that guy...his secre-
> tary said he was out of
> town.

Sam suddenly eyes the ballroom.

SAM'S POV

of the Ballroom. HETEROSEXUAL MEN dressed in
Brooks Brothers suits slow dance, not cheek to
cheek, around the Ballroom. As they dance,
most talk to one another. TWO BLACK MEN dance
only with each other. The ballroom, itself,
looks like an old gentlemen's club.

ANGLE

The sides of the ballroom. VARIOUS MEN watch
other men dance. One MAN stands whispering
into another MAN'S ear. Men, including TWO
BIG EATERS, stand near a buffet table filled
with male food: Oysters and large drumsticks.

WAITERS weave in and out delivering drinks. A
MAN checks himself out in a mirror. Another
MAN asks a MAN to dance. He nods and the two
begin to dance.

ANGLE

SAM watches the dancing.

ANGLE

A LINE OF WALL MOUNTED TELEPHONES

Various MEN talk on the phone.

> MAN ON PHONE
> Everybody stays there...the
> food is lousy, help sucks
> but everybody stays there...

> BENNY BERBEL ON PHONE
> Yeah, yeah I realize he's in
> a board of directors meet-
> ing, but tell him Benny
> Berbel is on the phone. I
> want to run something by him
> that I think he's gonna be
> interested in. I realize
> that, but uh—what's-what is
> your name? Sharon...Sharon
> help me out on this one will
> yeah. Get a message—I real-
> ize—Shar—see this from my
> point of view. Try to see
> this from my point of
> view...see everything from
> my point of view.

ANGLE

Men dancing.

REVERSE ANGLE

Cal and Sam watching dance floor.

ANGLE

A banquet table with MEN snacking food. A BIG
EATER talks to BIG EATER #2.

                              BIG EATER
          Tell me something. How do
          you talk about me behind my
          back. I'm curious.

                              BIG EATER #2
          Your back?

                              BIG EATER
          My back.

ANGLE

THE CROWDED BAR

A well-dressed GUY AT THE BAR in his mid-
thirties finishes a martini. He talks to the
BARTENDER.

                         GUY AT THE BAR
          Eddie, is that clock right?

                              BARTENDER
          Ah, yes, sir. It is.

                         GUY AT THE BAR
               (to himself)
          Ahh—I'll give him a few more
          minutes...
               (to Bartender)
          ...better give me another
          one.

                              BARTENDER
               (takes drink)
          Sure.

                         GUY AT THE BAR
          Wait, let me have the olive.
          Thank you.

MUSIC ENDS. Some men walk off the floor.
Others stay on. Constant chatter. A DISC
JOCKEY stands next to a compact high tech
turntable and places a platter. MUSIC BEGINS.
More men come on the floor with new partners.
Sam and Cal watch other Men move to floor.

Cal asks GEORGE, who looks like a banker, to
dance and the two begin to dance.

218

              CAL

George.

              GEORGE

Cal. How are you?

              CAL

How you doing? May I have
this dance?

              GEORGE

Sure.

Cal and George dance.

ANGLE

On the side seated on a couple of chairs.
SCHMOOZER #1 and SCHMOOZER #2 sit and talk.

              SCHMOOZER #1

See the game?

              SCHMOOZER #2

Oh, good game.

              SCHMOOZER #1

Great game.

              SCHMOOZER #2

Great. Great game. God. Wish
I could play like that.

              SCHMOOZER #1

We all wish we could play
like that.

              SCHMOOZER #2

Yeah, I know.

              SCHMOOZER #1

Saw the game?

              SCHMOOZER #2

No.

              SCHMOOZER #1

Na..me, neither.

ANGLE

Sam watches Men dance. A slick well-dressed
man, RAY PINDALLY, introduces himself to Sam.

219

They shake and talk into each other's ear
above the music and chatter.

> SAM (V.O.)
> The owner, Ray Pindally,
> came over and introduced
> himself to me. Told me his
> place was the latest trendy
> lunchtime ballroom, where
> guys like myself, obviously
> successful, danced to the
> old tunes, all the time
> talking business. I think he
> thought I was a tourist.

> RAY
> (To Sam)
> The powerful usually dance
> in their own spotlight. So
> be careful.

> SAM (V.O.)
> Spotlight, the powerful?

Sam spots the POWERFUL MAN on dance floor.

> SAM (V.O.)
> Tall lean man was no ques-
> tion about it, A powerful
> guy.

ANGLE

Dance floor. A SPOTLIGHT follows a DISTIN-
GUISHED-LOOKING MAN dancing with Another Man.
The other male dancers give these men free
rein and respect where they dance.

ANGLE

SAM stands near a group of MEN. Some men have
drinks in their hands, but most look towards
the dance floor.

The Schmoozer #2 stands next to a UPTIGHT
EXEC.

> SCHMOOZER #2
> Can I use you?

> UPTIGHT EXEC
>
> What for?

> SCHMOOZER #2
>
> Not important. Can I use
> you?

> UPTIGHT EXEC
>
> Of course you can use me.

ON SAM, slightly self conscious, looking
around for available men.

ANGLE

A SHORT, PUDGY MAN, quite a bit shorter than
Sam, looks at SAM from a distance and smiles.

ANGLE

SAM thinks the Short Man is looking at a man
behind him.

Another MAN approaches Sam, but asks the man
behind Sam to dance.

The Short Man approaches Sam and shyly asks
Sam...

> SHORT MAN
>
> Would you like to dance?

> SAM
>
> (Nervous)
>
> Sure.

The Two walk on the dance floor.

ANGLE

Dance Floor. The Short Man takes Sam's hand
and begins to lead. Sam, initially is confused
by who leads, but quickly adapts. The Short
Man is not a good dancer.

> SHORT MAN
>
> I've been coming here quite
> a long time...

> SAM (V.O.)
>
> This guy was pretty upfront.
> He told me he'd been coming
> (MORE)

221

                              SAM (V.O.) (CONT.)
                    to Ray's for years and
                    hadn't been asked to dance
                    with anyone for months.

                              SHORT MAN
                    I used to ask the powerful
                    guys to dance with me once
                    in a while, but I'd always
                    say the wrong things or step
                    on their...

The Short Man steps on Sam's foot. Sam reacts.

                              SHORT MAN
                    Sorry.

                              SAM
                    Uh-No, fine—it's fine.

He holds Sam's hand too tight. Sam reacts.

                              SHORT MAN
                    I'm sorry.

                              SAM
                    No, really

ANGLE

Cal, dancing with the same Partner, spots Sam
and winks.

ANGLE

Sam, self-consciously smiles back at Cal. Sam
and the Short Man dance.

                              SHORT MAN
                    I'm what they call dead meat
                    in this town. And most guys
                    who are seen dancing with
                    me, more than often, are
                    thought less of...so, if
                    you're smart, you'll stop
                    dancing with me right now.

                              SAM (V.O.)
                    I felt horrible. He wasn't
                    that bad a dancer. Are other
                    guys going to think I'm dead
                    meat because I'm dancing
                    with dead meat?

ANGLE

Other Men stare at Sam as if he's "dead meat."

ANGLE

Back to Sam and the Short Man.

> SAM (V.O.)
> Ah, So what? Then again, I
> was looking for a good job.
> This was not the time to
> make friends. Anyway, this
> guy gave me an out.

> SAM
> Actually, I am looking for a
> good job.

> SHORT MAN
> (Releasing his
> hand)
> Oh, well then I'll do you a
> favor and say good-bye.

The Short Man walks away towards the bar
leaving Sam alone on the dance floor. Uncom-
fortable, Sam walks off the floor.

ANOTHER BIG BAND SONG

ANGLE

Wall phones. Benny Berbel is still on the
phone with Sharon.

> BENNY BERBEL
> (Anxious)
> Sharon, hel-help me on this
> one, Sharon. You can help
> me. Ca-can-listen I'll tell
> you what. Help me I'll help
> you. What do you need. What
> do you need? You fly? I'll
> send you upgrades. In your
> name. You go it. You go to
> the theater? How bout—do you
> see Le Miz? I'll get you Le
> Miz tickets. Trevor is a
> friend of mine.

ANGLE

Another MAN checks himself out in the mirror.
Other Men watch others dance.

ANGLE

Guy At The Bar is still with the Bartender.

> GUY AT THE BAR
> I asked you if that clock
> was right, didn't I?

> BARTENDER
> Yes, sir.

> GUY AT THE BAR
> You haven't seen Don all
> day?

> BARTENDER
> No, sir.

> GUY AT THE BAR
> That's all right, he's gonna
> be here.

ANGLE

SCHMOOZER #1 is now at the wall of phones.

> SCHMOOZER #1 ON PHONE
> I don't know. I-I just feel
> uptight, under a lot of
> strain. I keep repeating the
> same patterns. Emotional re-
> runs, Doctor. I-

A man approaches to use that phone.

> SCHMOOZER #1 ON PHONE
> (upbeat)
> Hey, how are you! I'll just
> be a minute. Okay?
> (depressed into
> phone)
> Wh-where was I?

ANGLE

A HEAVY-SET EXEC and a SLENDER EXEC at the
bar, among other MEN as we hear in the b.g...
a TANGO.

224

                    HEAVY-SET EXEC
        You think this is the era of
        style over substance?

                    SLENDER EXEC
        Yes . . . and we're winning.

ANGLE

On Men's feet—dancing the tango—male shoe to
male shoe.

ANGLE

Dance floor. Sam and a SMOOTH-LOOKING MAN, a
good dancer and great dresser, dance a Tango.
The Smooth-looking Man leads.

                    SAM (V.O.)
        After dancing with a few
        other guys, I finally got
        into the swing of things.

                    SAM
        So, what do you do for a
        living?

                    SMOOTH-LOOKING MAN
        I'm not sure. That's not it
        exactly. I mean I draw a
        salary. A great salary.

                    SAM
        Well, if you don't want to
        talk about it, it's ok....

                    SMOOTH-LOOKING MAN
        It's not that, quite
        frankly, I don't even know
        what I do. You see, my boss
        hired me because he knew
        that others wanted me. So to
        prevent others from getting
        me, he hired me, now that
        he's got me he doesn't know
        quite what it is he wants to
        do with me.
             (swings out and
              into Sam's arms)
        Great benefits.

                    SAM
          Benefits?

                    SMOOTH-LOOKING MAN
          Benefits are very important.

                    SAM (V.O.)
          Said the man who didn't know
          what he did for a living.

ANGLE

On men's feet dancing side by side.

ANOTHER BIG BAND SONG

ANGLE

Buffet table. Eaters continue to nibble over a
dwindling lunch table. A balding MAN WITH
GLASSES nibbles.

                    MAN WITH GLASSES
          I'm not in a position to say
          yes. I can only say no. In
          fact, I've never been in a
          position to say yes.

ANGLE

Schmoozer #2 and Schmoozer #1 are seated in a
booth.

                    SCHMOOZER #2
          Did he mention my name?

                    SCHMOOZER #1
          What name?

                    SCHMOOZER #2
          My name.

                    SCHMOOZER #1
          No.

                    SCHMOOZER #2
          D-did you mention my name?

                    SCHMOOZER #1
          No.

>   SCHMOOZER #2
>   So, then there was no men-
>   tion really at all then?
>
>   SCHMOOZER #1
>   Of what?
>
>   SCHMOOZER #2
>   My name.
>
>   SCHMOOZER #1
>   Uh...no.

ANGLE

The dance floor. The DJ puts on a very SLOW
SONG.

>   SAM (V.O.)
>   It was in the middle of a
>   very slow dance that I found
>   out how much power the pow-
>   erful have.

The Powerful Guy goes to the DJ and makes him
change the record to an upbeat number. He
walks back onto the floor to resume dancing.
All the other men applaud his decision.

>   CAL
>   (passing the
>   Powerful Guy)
>   Great choice.
>
>   POWERFUL GUY
>   ...thanks.

Everyone continues dancing.

ANGLE

Short Guy curses himself and his bald spot in
the mirror.

ANGLE

The wall of phones. Benny Berbel is still on
the phone.

>   BENNY BERBEL
>   Okay, do me a favor. Just
>   get him one message to him.
>   (MORE)

> BENNY BERBEL (CONT.)
> Just get one message to
> him...see what he says. Tell
> him not to worry, his wife
> and kids are okay.

ANOTHER BIG BAND SONG.

ANGLE

The dance floor. Sam and a INSECURE LOOKING
EXEC DANCE. The Nervous Exec leads. They talk.

> SAM (V.O.)
> My day started to appear
> brighter. Much brighter. I
> danced with this man who
> seemed very excited about
> working with me.

> INSECURE EXEC
> We're looking for someone.
> Being very particular. We
> only want the best. You know
> that. I have this gut feel-
> ing. I think you're good.
> Could you start, let's say,
> next week?

> SAM
> Well, sure.

> INSECURE EXEC
> You can?

> SAM
> Yes, absolutely.

Insecure Exec grows even more nervous.

> SAM (V.O.)
> Then he confessed he had
> very little power and would
> have to confirm the offer
> with at least four execu-
> tives above him. He apolo-
> gized and promised to get
> back to me shortly.

Ray Pindally taps the Insecure Exec on the
shoulder.

228

                    RAY PINDALLY
          Excuse me, we seem to be
          having a slight problem with
          your credit card.

                    INSECURE EXEC
          Me?

                    RAY
          Yes, sir.

The Insecure Exec, embarrassed, lets go of
Sam...

                    INSECURE EXEC
          I have to take this call,
          excuse me.

And as the Exec and Ray exit...

                    RAY
          Stay out of the spot.

Sam, a tad embarrassed, stands in the middle
of the dance floor surrounded by dancing Men.

                    SAM (V.O.)
          Stay out of the spot? What
          spot? I must have been ten
          feet from the spotlight.

WE HEAR ANOTHER BIG BAND TUNE

THE BAR

Schmoozer #1 and Schmoozer #2 stand alongside
with the bar tab.

                    SCHMOOZER #2
          This is one me

                    SCHMOOZER #1
          Oh, no, no. Don't be ridicu-
          lous—

                    SCHMOOZER #2
          No, no, please. I insist. My
          turn.

                    SCHMOOZER #1
          No, this is my treat really.

                    SCHMOOZER #2
          No, no. Please. Your money's
          no good here.

ANGLE

Cal checks himself in the mirror.

                    CAL
               (memorizing)
          Lipton. Lipton. Jim Lipton.
          Big lips, ton of lips, ton
          of lips. Lipton. Lipton.

ANGLE

Guy at the Bar with Bartender.

                    GUY AT THE BAR
          Could I have mixed up the
          dates?

                    BARTENDER
          It's possible.

                    GUY AT THE BAR
          Well, who—whe—I'm sure he's
          gonna reschedule, you know.

                    BARTENDER
          Oh yeah, I'm sure.

ANGLE

Schmoozer #1 and Schmoozer #2 at the bar, now
dealing with their copy of the receipt.

                    SCHMOOZER #2
          It's mine.

                    SCHMOOZER #1
          No, you take this.

                    SCHMOOZER #2
          Please, it's done.

                    SCHMOOZER #1
               (mixing up credit
                card and receipt)
          This is uh—

                    SCHMOOZER #2
          It's done.
               (credit card)
          That's mine I believe.

                    SCHMOOZER #1
               (receipt)
          Oh, then this is mine.
               (to bartender)
          Say, George, two more. And
          this time, make sure it's my
          check.

                    SCHMOOZER #2
          Where were we?!

ANOTHER BIG BAND SONG—LATER

FIVE NEW MEN talk on the telephones.

ANGLE

Sam dances with a YOUNG BRIGHT EXEC, late
twenties. They trade off leading as if this
is a new dance. Sam tries to catch on to this
dance. He·actually enjoys it.

                    SAM (V.O.)
          I was then asked to take a
          spin by this executive, he
          had to be my age, who told
          me he was semi-retired. I
          couldn't believe it. He said
          he invented and successfully
          marketed the phrase "Have a
          Nice Day" years ago. Must
          have been so young. He was
          also testing out his new
          dance.

                    YOUNG BRIGHT EXEC
          You think this is a good
          dance?

                    SAM
          Yes, I do.

                    YOUNG BRIGHT EXEC
               (Excited)
          Do you think I could sell
          this dance?

                        SAM
          What dance?

                    YOUNG BRIGHT EXEC
                  (More excited)
          The dance we're doing.

                        SAM
          Oh, I don't know....

                    YOUNG BRIGHT EXEC
                  (In Sam's ear)
          Keep this dance between you
          and me, I think we have a
          winner.

                    SAM (V.O.)
          ...Winner.

The Young Bright Exec hurriedly leaves Sam.
The MUSIC STOPS and everyone applauds.

                    SAM (V.O.)
          Winner....and he ran out as
          if he discovered a new vac-
          cine.

CAL APPROACHES SAM.

                        CAL
                  (Proudly)
          Guess what? I just got a new
          job.

                        SAM
          Congratulations. You get
          more money?

ANOTHER BIG BAND SONG.

In the b.g., Men take new and old Partners on
the dance floor.

                        CAL
          Same pay. Same everything.
          Except this job is more
          geographically desirable. I
          just couldn't turn down
          something like this.
                  (Beat)
          Ask that guy right over
          there.

ANGLE

A rather overweight POMPOUS EXEC stands nurs-
ing a drink, watching the floor.

>   POMPOUS EXEC.
>   (to a passing exec)
>   Hey, how you doing?

ANGLE

BACK TO SAM AND CAL.

>   SAM
>   That guy?

>   CAL
>   Uh-hm

>   SAM
>   Really?

>   CAL
>   Yes.

>   CUT TO:

DANCE FLOOR.

SAM and the Pompous Exec dance. Sam leads.

>   SAM (V.O.)
>   I danced with a man I nor-
>   mally would never talk to if
>   it wasn't for Cal telling me
>   he was important. Didn't
>   trust his smile. I didn't
>   trust his tempo. His atten-
>   tion span scaled no more
>   than two seconds.

>   POMPOUS EXEC
>   So, you-uh-you have a wife?

>   SAM
>   No.

>   POMPOUS EXEC
>   I have one.

>   SAM
>   Ahh.

233

                    POMPOUS EXEC
          Kids?

                    SAM
          No.

                    POMPOUS EXEC
          I have a boy and girl.
          House?

                    SAM
          No, I rent.

                    POMPOUS EXEC
          Oh, you rent?

                    SAM
          Yeah.

                    POMPOUS EXEC
          You know we have a lot in
          common.

                    SAM (V.O.)
          If there was a revolution, I
          would have to kill him. Any
          kind of revolution. But I
          needed a job.

                    SAM
          Look, I'd love to talk to
          you...uh-uh

                    POMPOUS EXEC
          Ed....

                    SAM
          I'd love to talk to you, Ed,
          in your office...

                    POMPOUS EXEC
          Yeah, well, none of my real
          business is done in the
          office. Most of my real
          business is done here on the
          dance floor.

                    SAM
          Well, let's talk right
          here...

                    POMPOUS EXEC
                 (Letting go of his
                  arm)
          Oh, I would love to talk,
          but I'm scheduled to talk to
          Tom Hartlow of Hartlow In-
          ternational in about—um—hoo-
          hoo—two minutes. So listen,
          you say hello to your good-
          looking family of yours.

                    SAM
          I don't have a family...

                    POMPOUS EXEC
          Yeah, we'll talk soon.

ANGLE

The Pompous Exec races over to HARTLOW, another exec.

ANGLE

Sam stands alone on the floor. He looks at his
watch. Self-consciously, he walks towards the
bar area and turns around towards the dance
area. Sam recognizes Peter.

ANGLE

The POWERFUL GUY and PETER, an exec in his
thirties, dance in a spotlight.

                    SAM (V.O.)
          I was about to leave Ray's
          and make that job interview
          when I spotted Peter, my
          best friend from my last
          job, dancing with the power-
          ful guy in the spotlight.
          The powerful guy was a great
          dancer.

The Powerful Guy spins Peter around three or
four times.

ANGLE

Sam hovers over Peter's shoulder. He taps him.

                    SAM
               (Excited)
          Peter?

                    PETER
               (Looks at him
                oddly)
          Excuse me?

                    SAM
          Peter. How are you? I don't
          mean to interrupt...

                    PETER
               (Covering)
          I'm sorry, my name isn't
          Peter. I think you must have
          me mixed up...

                    SAM
          Mixed up? Come on, it's Sam
          Logan. Fabtek Corporation.

                    SAM (V.O.)
          He looked at me as if I was
          a non-person, an alien,
          another species. Of course,
          he knew me. We always had
          lunch together. He always
          ordered meat loaf. We traded
          ball scores. We once dated
          the same secretary.

                    SAM
               (re-approaching
                Peter)
          Excuse me, could I talk to
          you for a second?

                    PETER
          Look, Mr. Logan, I think you
          have me mixed up with some-
          one else, so if you don't
          mind...

          Peter and the Powerful Guy quickly jettison
          into another direction.

                    PETER
               (to Powerful Guy)
          So, I understand that your
          wife's name is Bonny also?

                    POWERFUL GUY
          That's correct, but let's
          talk business.
                        PETER
          Uh-uh. All right.

ANGLE

Sam, looking wiped out and defeated, walks
slowly towards the exit through the bar. As he
is about to exit....

                    POWERFUL GUY (O.S.)
                (calling)
            Mr. Logan?

Sam stops and turns.

ANGLE

The Powerful Guy hurries through the crowded
bar area and catches up to him. The crowd,
like the sea, parts for the Powerful Guy.

                    POWERFUL GUY
          I'm Dick Tratten of the
          Tratten Group.

                    SAM (V.O.)
          I knew the company. Great
          reputation.

                    POWERFUL GUY
          I don't know you, but I'm
          impressed with your honesty.

We hear another big band song begin.

                    POWERFUL GUY
                (milking the beat)
          Like to dance?

                    SAM
                (Beat)
          Yes.

ANGLE

The Distinguished-looking Man guides Sam onto
the crowded dance floor. The other dancers
APPLAUD as the Distinguished-looking Man leads

237

Sam under the spotlight.. as they and everyone
else dance around the room.

> SAM (V.O.)
>
> Well, I'm pleased to report,
> I danced and danced and
> danced with Dick Tratten of
> the Tratten Group. We have a
> lot in common... and the
> rest is history.

FADE OUT

BIBLIOGRAPHY

Aristotle, *Poetics* translated by Richard Janko. Hackett Publishing Company, Indianapolis/Cambridge. 1987.

Armer, Alan A., *Writing the* Screenplay. Wadsworth, Publishing Company, Belmont, California. 1993.

Blacker, Iwrin R. *The Elements of Screenwriting*. Collier Books, MacMillan Publishers. 1986.

Lajos, Egri, *The Art of Dramatic Writing*. Simon & Schuster, New York. 1960.

E.M. Forster, *Aspects of the Novel*. Harcourt, Brace and World, New York. 1927

Halperin, Michael, *Writing Great Characters: The Psychology of Character Development in Screenplays*. Lone Eagle Publishing Co., Los Angeles, California. 1996.

Johnson, Lincoln F., *Film: Space, Time, Light and Sound*. Holt, Rinehart and Winston, New York. 1974.

Jung, C.G., *Psychological Types,* a revision by R.F.C. Hull of the translation by H.G. Baynes. Princeton University Press, Princeton, New Jersey. 1971.

Kazan, Eli, *A Life*. Anchor Books, New York. 1989.

King, Viki, *How to Write a Movie in 21* Days. Harper Perennial, New York. 1988.

Lawson, John Howard, *Theory and Technique of Playwriting and Screenwriting*. Garland Publishers, New York. 1985.

Lucey, Paul, *Story Sense*. McGraw-Hill, New York. 1996.

Lumet, Sidney, *Making Pictures*. Knopf, New York. 1995.

Mehring, Margaret, *The Screenplay: A Blend of Film Form and* Content. Focal Press, Boston, Massachusetts. 1990.

Perret, Gene, *How to Write & Sell Your Sense of Humor*. Writer's Digest Books, Cincinnati, Ohio. 1982.

Seger, Linda, *Making a Good Script Great*. Dodd, Mead & Company, New York. 1987.

Shaw, Harry, *Concise Dictionary of Literary Terms*. McGraw-Hill Paperbacks, New York. 1972.

Stanislavski, Constantin, *The Actor Prepares*, translated by Elizabeth Reynolds Hapgood. Theater Arts Books, New York. 1948

INDEX

BOOKS FOR WRITERS

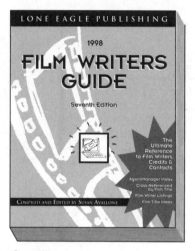

1998 FILM WRITERS GUIDE Seventh Edition

Compiled and Edited by Susan Avallone

Over 7300 screenwriters, 28,000 film titles and listings of unproduced screenplays.

$70.00
ISBN 0-943728-98-3
8.5 x 11, approx. 675 pp.

WRITING GREAT CHARACTERS
The Psychology of Character Development
By Michael Halperin, Ph.D.

A book for all writers, from the expert who is looking to polish his techniques to the novice who wants to learn the craft from an expert.

$19.95
ISBN 0-943728-79-7
original trade paper
6 x 9, 196 pp.

BOOKS FOR WRITERS

$16.95
ISBN 0-943728-88-6
original trade paper
6 x 9, 170 pp.

HOW TO ENTER SCREENPLAY CONTESTS . . . AND WIN!
An Insider's Guide To Selling Your Screenplay To Hollywood
By Erik Joseph
This book contains comprehensive listings of screenplay contests to enter as well as provides insider information, testimonials and seasoned advice for writers ready to make their first pitch. Learn how to write a well-structured screenplay.

TOP SECRETS: SCREENWRITING
By Jurgen Wolff
and Kerry Cox
"TOP SECRETS is an authentic stand-out. The combination of biographies, analyses, interviews and actual script samples is a real winner."
–Professor Richard Walter, UCLA

$21.95
ISBN 0-943728-50-9
original trade paper
6 x 9, 342 pp.

ABOUT THE AUTHOR

Linda Cowgill DeCrane is a screen and television writer who has taught screenwriting at the American Film Institute and Loyola Marymount University in Los Angeles. Her feature *Opposing Force* was released by Orion Pictures in 1986. She has written for such television shows as "Quincy," "Life Goes On" and "The Young Riders." She won the Genesis Award for her "Call of the Wild" episode of *Life Goes On*. She has a B.A. and M.F.A. from UCLA. Her student film, *Froggy went a'Courtin'*, won a UCLA Jim Morrison Award for best short film. She lives in Santa Monica with her husband and daughter.